'*Success Stories from Secondary Foreign Langua[...]* a seminal text for all reflective practitioners who [...] communicative environment a stimulating, effecti[...] [...] day in and day out. Each story offers insight into engaged, creative practice, raising pertinent questions and providing possible solutions for all those navigating the diverse challenges of the current MFL landscape.'

– Anneli McLachlan, MFL educator, consultant and writer

'This book is testament to the invaluable and irreplaceable working partnerships developed by providers of teacher training and schools, facilitated by the beginner teacher. It is an informed collection of research-based investigations which provides current guidance to all language teachers in leading the teaching of languages during the changes in curricula, assessment and value of languages in the pupils' educational experience.'

– Andy Jackson, Head of Languages, Gladesmore Community School

'All colleagues involved in languages education – trainees, heads of department and teacher educators alike – will find this publication fascinating reading. The wide range of topics covered are timely in how they deal with recent developments in the national curriculum, and offer tremendous insight into ongoing concerns in language teaching, such as primary–secondary transition, assessment and building resilience in school language departments. The practical ideas and links to research offer inspiration for transforming language teaching practice.'

– Ruth Bailey, teaching fellow and PGCE director, Graduate School of Education, University of Bristol.

'This book is full of ideas that remind the Language teaching community how important our work is, and how collaboration and creative planning reinforce principles we espouse: the motivation of lifelong Language learners and of resilient Language teachers in our classrooms. The examples and reflections are highly relevant to elements of the new curriculum and exams. Furthermore, they are realistic and show how professionals working together tackle our ongoing challenges positively.'

– Steven Fawkes, Association for Language Learning

Success Stories from Secondary Foreign Languages Classrooms

Success Stories from Secondary Foreign Languages Classrooms

Models from London school partnerships with universities

Edited by Colin Christie and Caroline Conlon

is an imprint of

First published in 2016 by the UCL Institute of Education Press, University College London, 20 Bedford Way, London WC1H 0AL

www.ucl-ioe-press.com

British Library Cataloguing in Publication Data:
A catalogue record for this publication is available from the British Library

ISBNs
978-1-85856-788-4 (paperback)
978-1-85856-789-1 (PDF eBook)
978-1-85856-790-7 (ePub eBook)
978-1-85856-791-4 (Kindle eBook)

Typeset by Quadrant Infotech (India) Pvt Ltd
Printed by CPI Group (UK) Ltd, Croydon, CR0 4YY
Cover ©Rawpixel.com/Shutterstock

Contents

List of figures and tables

Abbreviations

Abbreviations are generally written in full the first time they are used in each section but are reproduced here for convenience. MFL, PGCE and GCSE appear repeatedly and, as widely used terms in the English secondary school setting, are not written out in full every time.

AfL	Assessment for learning
ALL	Association for Language Learning
BFI	British Film Institute
CILT	The National Centre for Languages (closed in 2011)
CPD	Continuing professional development
EAL	English as an additional language
EBacc	The English Baccalaureate. This is a school performance measure that indicates how many pupils achieve a grade C or above in the core academic subjects (under review during 2016) at key stage 4 in any government-funded school.
ELT	English language teaching
FLs	Foreign languages
GCSE	General Certificate of Education
GTP	Graduate Teacher Programme
HE	Higher Education
HEI	Higher Education Institution
HoD	Head of department
ICT	Information and communications technology
IOE	UCL Institute of Education
ITE	Initial teacher education
IU	Intercultural Understanding (a KS2 Framework objective)
KAL	Knowledge about Language (a KS2 Framework objective)
KCL	King's College London
KS2	Key stage 2 (Years 3 to 6 in English schools, ages 7–11)
KS3	Key stage 3 (Years 7 to 9 in English schools, ages 11–14)
KS4	Key stage 4 (Years 10 to 11 in English schools, ages 14–16)
LA	Local authority
LEA	Local education authority
LLS	Language Learning Strategies (a KS2 Framework objective)
MFL	Modern foreign languages

M-Level	Master's-level
NC	National Curriculum
NQTs	Newly qualified teachers
PGCE	Postgraduate Certificate in Education
PPP	Present-practice-produce (3Ps)
QTS	Qualified Teacher Status
RQTs	Recently qualified teachers
SATs	National Curriculum tests in English primary schools (often referred to as SATS)
SLA	second language acquisition
SLT	Senior leadership team
SMT	Senior management team
TL	Target language

Acknowledgements

This book is the product of a joint effort by a team of foreign languages educators from across London. They share a commitment to reflective practice to ensure the best for their secondary school-age learners, and we should like to thank them all for that commitment and for the time they have devoted to this project. Life in education is busy, but this group of people have managed to find the time to collaborate and share their work in each of their chapters. As editors, we should like to give Jane Jones a particular mention; her support and encouragement as an experienced, widely published writer have been invaluable.

Thank you also to Ann Swarbrick for her interest and support. It is gratifying to know that someone with so much experience and wisdom values our project. Finally to one another, thank you! Mutual respect, friendship and a shared sense of humour are all essential ingredients when adding to an already challenging workload. It has reminded us both how important it is to keep making space for the things you believe in and want to do.

Thanks also to the Saint-Exupéry-d'Agay Estate for their kind permission to reproduce the image in Chapter 5.

Contributors

Marian Carty is course coordinator for the Secondary PGCE Languages programme at Goldsmiths, University of London. Prior to joining Goldsmiths, she was the course leader for the Modern Foreign Languages (MFL) PGCE at the University of Cumbria, London Campus. As a classroom practitioner, she was seconded as a teacher fellow to Homerton College, Cambridge, to develop the London Borough of Croydon's Graded Objectives in Modern Languages Scheme and went on to work as an MFL adviser in the London Boroughs of Merton and Greenwich with a focus on Graded Assessment. She was later employed as course leader for the MFL PGCE Secondary and Primary BA QTS at the Roehampton Institute of Education and was also a teacher liaison officer at the National Centre for Languages (CILT). Marian is interested in promoting learner use of the target language, fostering creativity, catering for the diverse needs of learners with special educational needs and advancing social justice.

Colin Christie is a lecturer in Languages in Education and subject leader for the PGCE Languages course at the UCL Institute of Education, London. He has held a number of advisory positions, including as a key stage 3 consultant, and has produced teaching resources in a variety of media. He has worked in schools and colleges in different roles, such as a languages development project coordinator in a language college and as head of department. His PhD thesis was on the subject of spontaneous learner target language talk in the languages classroom.

Simon Coffey is a senior lecturer in education (modern foreign languages) at King's College London, where he teaches on the MFL PGCE and is programme director of the MA in Language and Cultural Diversity. He taught foreign languages for many years and his research interests are language pedagogies, motivation, the use of discourse analytic approaches to understand individuals' investment in language learning across the lifespan and how to encourage a broader conception of the value of language learning. He has been the UK lead in several European Union (EU)-funded projects and has published widely on language autobiographies and teacher professional development.

Caroline Conlon is a lecturer in Languages in Education at UCL Institute of Education, London, where she teaches on both the PGCE Languages and Master of Teaching (MTeach) programmes, supporting new and experienced teachers with a wide range of Master's-level research. After working as a languages teacher in London schools for many years, she went on to further study and worked with the Widening Participation team at King's College London. In 2004, she joined the Languages in Education team at CILT where she was involved in a number of national and regional projects to support the development of both KS2 and KS3 languages across London's 33 local authorities (LAs). She also taught on the CILT Graduate Teacher Programme (GTP) before moving to UCL in 2011.

Fotini Diamantidaki has, for the past seven years, been a lecturer on the PGCE Languages course and other teacher education routes at the UCL Institute of Education, London. Prior to joining the PGCE team, she was a secondary school teacher of French, a mentor and a coordinator for A-level and ICT in London secondary schools. Since the completion of her MA and PhD on the integration of literature in the language classroom in combination with the use of Internet and digital technologies, teacher development in this area has become a fundamental strand of her teacher educator role.

Anna Lise Gordon was an MFL teacher in schools in London and Surrey, and an LA advisery teacher, before moving into initial teacher education (ITE) at St Mary's University in Twickenham. During her recent doctoral research inquiry, Anna Lise explored the resilience of early career teachers, including over 50 MFL PGCE trainee teachers working in a range of London schools. She focused on the challenges to the resilience of these early career teachers, but also explored what nurtures and sustains their resilience in the initial stages of the teaching profession. She found that the inspiration and positive support of the mentor and the wider MFL team were key factors for many of these trainee teachers. This led her to consider what makes a resilient MFL team, able to sustain itself in challenging times and provide the best possible context to support MFL teachers and learners.

Jane Jones is Head of MFL Teacher Education (PGCE and MA) in the Department of Education, Communication and Society, King's College London (KCL). She previously taught languages for many years in secondary schools and mentored trainee teachers for King's and other higher education institutions throughout her school teaching career. Jane has also been active in promoting primary MFL, working with primary schools to help develop their skills and provision. Her main research interests are formative assessment (she is a member of the KCL Assessment for Learning Group), primary–secondary transition, Comparative and International Education and 'Teachers as Researchers'. She is particularly keen to promote the pupil voice in a paradigm of teacher research that engages the students in a dialogue with their teachers about their learning. Jane believes that teachers' research capability and enthusiasm for research can be most effectively developed and encouraged in Initial Teacher Education where a university research culture can support the necessary skills.

Shirley Lawes was, until recently, subject leader for PGCE Languages at the UCL Institute of Education, London. Her work now is largely as a research supervisor, independent trainer and researcher in language teaching and teacher development. She has published widely on a number of aspects of foreign language teaching and learning, teacher education and broader educational issues. Her recent research and curriculum development work has been with the British Film Institute on the use of short films in the foreign languages classroom. In 2008 she was awarded the *Chevalier dans l'Ordre des Palmes Académiques* by the French Ministry of Education for her career-long contribution to the promotion of French language and culture.

Glennis Pye has worked at St Mary's University in Twickenham since 2009. She teaches on the PGCE Secondary Modern Languages programme and the undergraduate and postgraduate primary programmes for trainee teachers. She continues to teach French and Spanish at a local secondary school and has also recently authored a new French course for KS3. In the past, Glennis worked in a range of roles related to language learning and teaching. After studying French and Spanish at university she spent several years working abroad as an English language teacher in a number of school settings and as an ELT adviser for Cambridge University Press. She later trained and worked as a lexicographer in the UK, contributing to bilingual and monolingual dictionaries for learners of English, before teaching French and Spanish in the secondary school sector.

Judith Rifeser is a teacher–researcher. An experienced primary, secondary and higher education practitioner in MFL and EAL, she was, until recently, head of KS5 German, CPD facilitator and subject mentor for PGCE students and newly qualified teachers in German and Spanish at Orleans Park School, Twickenham. Before completing her PGCE, she taught Spanish and Italian as a junior lecturer at the Johns Hopkins University (USA), where she also contributed to the Austro-American educational documentary *See You Soon Again*. She completed her MPhil in European Literature and Culture at the University of Cambridge (2010) and was recently awarded the University of Roehampton Vice-Chancellor Scholarship to undertake research full-time toward her PhD in cultural studies. Judith's research interests include practice-as-research (both in cultural studies and in language teaching and learning), the use of audiovisual resources, gender studies, phenomenology, film studies and philosophy of education.

Foreword

Ann Swarbrick

The diverse population of London schools provides a very rich environment in which languages teachers (and, in particular, those language teachers just starting out) can develop their skills. Teaching in any city requires commitment and determination to keep pupils engaged in the learning process but the inner city has a particular mix of pupils that requires the teacher to demonstrate exceptional levels of resilience, creativity and ingenuity. The contributors to this book are all based in higher education institutions (HEIs) in London, training student teachers within this context. All the HEIs have created very strong partnerships with the schools in which they work. These schools provide quality teaching placements for student teachers and have also built a much closer working relationship around the education research agenda. As a result, there now exists a strong corpus of work that has been tried and tested in schools' languages classrooms.

The contributions in this book represent an excellent cross-section of the research being undertaken within the languages education academic community in English schools. All of the authors work with schools on a daily basis, supporting their student teachers within the school and university context. Since much of the training year is completed in-school, there is close liaison between school languages departments and academics within the higher education institutions. All of the research described in the book is a result of these collaborative relationships which means that it is both close to the classroom and to the experience of teachers and student teachers.

Through the different case studies, you will see that learning languages in London schools is an enormously exciting undertaking, and learning to teach languages in urban settings is one of the most rewarding challenges anyone could embark upon.

Ann Swarbrick
Former President of the Association for
Language Learning

Introduction

Colin Christie and Caroline Conlon

Genuine partnerships

'The London Providers' is the name given to the Greater London university initial teacher education (ITE) providers. The London Providers' commitment to cooperation and collaboration prevails over the competitive nature of the education sector and ensures that mutually supportive relationships benefit the wider agenda, namely that of good teachers teaching modern foreign languages (MFL) well in schools.

The London Providers work with many of London's 400-plus secondary schools in (often) long-standing, mutually enriching relationships, with ongoing discussions about practice informed by advances in theory and grounded in classroom experience. These university–school partnerships create an environment that fosters reflective practice, encouraging a spirit of exploration and experimentation. The partnerships are enriched by London's dynamic, diverse, multilingual profile, comparable to that of many other urban settings.

Due to the current government's preference for school-based training routes, the benefits of the university contribution to teacher education are under the spotlight. It therefore feels appropriate and timely to highlight what successful university–school partnerships can offer to the nurturing of MFL, and to share the strengths and successes that these relationships bring to our subject. All of this is especially important for a subject that still endures a risk of fragility with issues around student uptake and teacher shortages.

Theory and practice informing each other

The Postgraduate Certificate in Education (PGCE) Master's-level programmes of the London Providers form the basis of the partnership successes described in this book. They provide a framework for all MFL teachers (whether in training, newly or recently qualified or experienced teachers in their role as subject mentors) to collaborate and experiment in their lessons, reflect on their successes and use theory to inform their conclusions. These vibrant discussions and interactions, in turn, form the basis of a community of pedagogues developing shared understandings. This is particularly crucial in a period when many of the networks on which we previously relied to share ideas about developments in our subject have been cut back, with, for example, the closure of the National Centre for Languages (CILT) and the reduction of local authority (LA) advisory services. With a decreasing number of teachers in training and with the variety of routes available to those wishing to study to become teachers, communication is challenging but never more important.

All contributors remain passionate about theory–practice relationships and aim to share examples of successes in the classroom that have emerged during constant exchanges of ideas and reflections. As Jane Jones states in Chapter 1, the supposed divide between theory and practice is 'false and unnecessary'. It is the aim of all the providers to promote the development of teachers who not only teach well but are able to reflect critically on policy and practice and innovate to take their subject forward. In the words of Shirley Lawes, the PGCE programmes aim to encourage student teachers to develop simultaneously as 'competent practitioners, principled professionals and educational thinkers'.

Challenges and opportunities

The teaching of foreign languages in secondary schools has historically faced a number of challenges, many of which continue to perplex professionals charged with the successful teaching of the subject. A previous response to such challenges was to remove it from the statutory key stage 4 (KS4) curriculum in 2004, which resulted in a reduction in the number of MFL teachers in schools and led to concerns about languages uptake in the UK. Recent policy decisions, however, indicate that policymakers seem keen for languages to feature in a broad and balanced 11–16 offer. The revised school performance measures (Progress 8 and Attainment 8), and potentially EBacc in the future, include languages in an attempt to support increased uptake, and initial signs are positive: languages are back!

As well as perennial debates around topics such as the role of grammar, pupil use of the target language and the interpretation of the communicative approach, new challenges and opportunities have resulted from policy changes. These include ensuring progression across phases, with the National Curriculum for Languages (see http://tinyurl.com/jryuc82) cementing the statutory seven-year foreign language learning programme across KS2–KS3. The subject community is also managing further new demands, such as effective use of literary texts at KS3, assessment without levels, translation and dictation and recruitment and retention of language teachers against a backdrop of a potential teacher shortage in the very near future. Furthermore, this current National Curriculum could be seen as a desire by policymakers to return to a more traditional approach – that is, a return to elements of grammar translation, which some perceive as a regressive step in comparison to the communicative approaches advocated in recent years.

This is, therefore, a decisive moment for a 'bottom-up' approach, for teachers and teacher educators to come together to establish some shared understanding as they interpret programmes of study within the communicative language teaching ethos. As a more limited description of what foreign language teaching and learning should look like in schools, the new National Curriculum and its attendant challenges have reinforced the need for teacher educators and school teachers to join forces to plan and assert a credible and exciting offer. Communication and collaboration are powerful tools, as schools and universities pool resources to find solutions.

As initial teacher educators who work with student teachers and subject mentors across London's 33 boroughs and outlying counties, we are aware, then, that there are success stories to be told. In this book, we aim to share some examples of best practice from across the London ITE partnerships. Each of the case studies analyses and celebrates successful practice informed by theoretical perspectives. In a context of ever-changing policy and ever-evolving theory, we aim to highlight practical and creative solutions to some of our most challenging issues.

About this book

This book is not only about success stories. It also aims to strengthen our community of practitioners who are charged with responding quickly and creatively to this complex landscape. For subject leaders, experienced and new teachers and student teachers at the start of their languages careers, the book has something to offer. It promotes ways of working in university–school partnerships that draw on mutual strengths, bringing together theory and practice in realizable ways. There is a range of voices from different partners, with the result that the book does not offer a one-size-fits-all set of solutions, but rather uses success stories as a means to promote discussion, reflection and strategy development.

The London Providers have shared examples from within their partnerships, and we have organized the contributions into two strands: continuing professional development (CPD) and creative classroom practice, moving from consideration of more overarching issues to classroom-based pedagogy. Each chapter can be approached as a stand-alone read. The book represents a forum for individual teachers in schools in London, and indeed MFL teachers in other urban locales, to share their knowledge and expertise with the wider MFL community.

Chapter synopses

Chapter 1: Teachers as emergent critical researchers of practice
Jane Jones, King's College London
There is growing support for teacher research to take a central role in CPD entitlement and for teachers to have opportunities to pursue their own personalized professional development needs. In this chapter I argue that teachers' critical research skills can be most effectively developed in the early stages of teacher training. It is at this stage that new teachers are especially open-minded, curious and naturally inclined toward exploration when they are learning to discern 'what works' and 'in what circumstances' in their first teaching experiences. The training that needs to frame this experience seeks to promote student teachers as critically reflective practitioners and researchers, the two going hand-in-hand.

In school, student teachers' practical try-outs are encouraged and supported by their mentors; and in the university setting, reflection and research are given structure and dedicated time. With training in research skills, new teachers can very quickly become emergent competent researchers of their own practice and that of others, albeit in a modest way. In this chapter, I explore the opportunities for research on a training course and present a series of mini-profiles of recently qualified teachers (RQTs). These teachers, inspired by the research focus of the PGCE, have successfully undertaken creditable classroom research in urban schools in the London area that has had a positive impact on their subject knowledge and practice. I present accounts of their research and show how the desire to research has become part of their teacher identities.

Chapter 2: Creating and nurturing resilient MFL teams
Anna Lise Gordon, St Mary's University London
This chapter focuses on the importance of resilience in MFL teams to promote teacher well-being and progression in pupil learning in a constantly changing MFL educational climate. Insights from some of the current literature and research around teacher well-being, including resilience, form the contextual background to this exploration of some of the key issues faced by MFL teams. The importance of responding to the emotional aspects of working together is considered, and particular attention is given to the induction of

newcomers into a team, especially newly qualified teachers (NQTs), as well as approaches to nurturing and developing an MFL team over time. The chapter includes reference to case studies from successful MFL departments, identifying challenges and solutions-focused approaches to a number of key issues. The chapter concludes with suggestions for activities for the MFL team to review and reflect on resilience in a positive way. The strong focus on the benefits of collaboration between MFL colleagues and initial teacher training providers is also highlighted.

Chapter 3: Making the most of the mixed-experience Year 7 classroom
Caroline Conlon, UCL Institute of Education
Since the 19 KS2 Pathfinder pilots in 1999, secondary school teachers have been faced with the challenge of building on the prior learning and knowledge from a growing and increasingly diverse foreign language (FL) offer in primary schools. In September 2014, languages were made a statutory requirement at KS2. In this chapter I will argue that this rich mix of prior foreign language learning is an opportunity rather than a threat, that an assumption of no prior knowledge cannot be the answer, and that it is possible to capitalize on the mixed KS2 FL experiences to ensure engagement and progress for all.

The 2013 National Curriculum (see http://tinyurl.com/jryuc82) and revised GCSE represent a chance to revisit some fundamental questions: Which languages should be offered at KS3? Could a less teacher-centred approach be a way forward from the outset? Could the time be right to shift our focus from content to skills? Do we need to reconceptualize the notions of progression in FL teaching and learning? The questions raised have begun to be addressed in practice by one inner-city FL teacher who will share her responses thus far. The student comments throughout the chapter are provided by a small focus group in her Year 7 French class.

Chapter 4: Using literature in the key stage 3 modern foreign languages classroom
Fotini Diamantidaki, UCL Institute of Education
This chapter demonstrates the potential for using literature to enhance learning in the KS3 foreign language classroom, enabling learners to go beyond the instrumental functions of the target language. It considers how the effective use of authentic texts has the potential to reinforce and develop reading skills in particular, alongside the strengthening of all language skills to improve learners' overall linguistic proficiency. More specifically,

the chapter examines the results of a UCL Institute of Education literature project involving PGCE student teachers and their language learners in schools during the academic year 2014/15.

The results are presented here to demonstrate how literature can be integrated into topics within existing schemes of work rather than as an add-on or one-off task, allowing teachers and learners to focus on developing language skills through the use of authentic literary materials over a series of lessons. The chapter also examines the rewards, challenges and future implications of the project.

Chapter 5: Teaching literature to promote creativity in language learning
Simon Coffey, King's College London

In this chapter, I first consider the recent impetus around the construct of creativity as a guiding concept in language teaching. There is still some uncertainty about what is understood by the term and what it can look like in different teaching and learning contexts. I then explore the renewed focus on using stories in the language classroom at a time when the most recent National Curriculum has re-emphasized the teaching of literature: not just the set texts so familiar to sixth form teachers, but also a broader range of literary texts that can appeal to younger learners. I will show how literature and creativity can support each other, with reference to a teaching sequence designed and taught by one modern languages teacher.

The sequence addresses fundamental questions about the purposes of language teaching and the appeal of language as an aesthetic and cultural value, extending the dominant paradigm of communicative utility. The creative use of literature allows different layers of language and intercultural, personal and social development to be integrated flexibly into language teaching, which can be especially helpful in contexts of rich cultural diversity such as in London schools.

Chapter 6: Breaking out: The use of film in the MFL classroom
Colin Christie and Shirley Lawes, UCL Institute of Education

This chapter examines the advantages of using film in foreign language lessons, and shows how this can be exploited to meet the requirements of the new National Curriculum (see http://tinyurl.com/jryuc82). It demonstrates how film can address a variety of objectives, such as the provision of cultural input, the development of listening skills and creative speaking and writing. Film need not be separate from a programme of study and reserved for special occasions, but rather can be integrated into lesson planning so that it contributes to learners' progress in the language. The case is made for exploiting film material and responding creatively to it in the target language, enhancing skills in language production.

The theoretical aspects are supported by a description of good practice in this area. This includes an outline of the film project that is part of the UCL Institute of Education's PGCE Languages course in collaboration with the British Film Institute (BFI). There is also an account of a former PGCE student teacher's use of the materials produced for this project in the classroom.

Chapter 7: Translation in secondary school languages teaching
Glennis Pye, St Mary's University London

This chapter examines the use of translation in the teaching of languages. It begins by describing the changing landscape in secondary school education in England that makes the use of translation an area of interest. It traces the fluctuations in attitudes toward the use of translation in language teaching, from the time of the Grammar Translation method to the present, and considers to what extent current perceptions of the use of translation mirror related theory on the subject. It goes on to discuss practical ways in which effective and engaging translation activities might be developed in response to the new National Curriculum requirements (see http://tinyurl.com/jryuc82).

Chapter 8: Formative assessment as context for developing autonomous language use and language learning
Marian Carty, Goldsmiths, University of London and Judith Rifeser, Orleans Park School

This chapter explores the collaborative work between Marian Carty, coordinator of the Goldsmiths PGCE MFL course, and the MFL department at a partnership school, Orleans Park. Their joint work is captured in a case study of the research project undertaken by Judith Rifeser, the school's MFL teacher, in a GCSE German classroom. For over ten years, the department had been using an interactive approach that places the target language at the very centre of learning, but when it came to feedback on written work, teachers reverted to the use of English. They agreed this was a missed opportunity for learning.

In response, assessment tools were devised to raise learners' grammatical awareness and understanding. These tools were used by both pupils and teachers to identify strengths and areas for development in the learners' writing. This approach resulted in improved accuracy in their written work to ensure excellent results in their GCSE controlled assessments, and, in the future, in their end of course GCSE writing exams. Some of the questions explored in this chapter with reference to theory and school practice are: How can learners be involved in reflection and review to make them more confident and independent learners? How can assessment and feedback be most useful in terms of language learning, and most efficient in terms of teacher time expended, while taking into account both the process and the outcome? How can the success criteria be made explicit and integrated into teaching?

Part One

Continuing professional
development (CPD)

1

Teachers as emergent critical researchers of practice

Jane Jones

The context: Student teachers learning to conduct research in MFL

Teachers instinctively and automatically reflect on their practice every day. They might not notice this but, invariably, the events of the day or week will generate questions, concerns and ideas, and plans will start to take shape in their minds. Sometimes ideas form privately, when marking some work, for instance, or later at home; and sometimes the ideas that surface are shared and developed collaboratively with a colleague in the staffroom or even in the photocopying room (a fertile discussion area!). Ideas are the first stage of a thinking process that is almost second nature to teachers and that could lead to research, given the right time and space. In such circumstances, teachers can be well positioned to give insightful, valid and invaluable accounts of pedagogical processes and practices in their classrooms. Indeed, given teachers' natural classroom habitus, working constantly with data, this makes them '*ipso facto* researchers into their own practice' (Bryant, 1996: 115).With the trend toward evidence-based practice, and in an era of unprecedented accountability, teachers are increasingly called to give valid accounts of what works well in their classrooms, and under what conditions. The potential to create these accounts can be nurtured at the initial teacher education (ITE) stage, where critical reflection frames the whole process and where, crucially, teachers have time to reflect.

In this respect, experienced teachers, rightly perhaps, bemoan the fact that they have little time to undertake such investigations, although a small number of schools have included teacher research activities in their professional development programme. Otherwise, time and space for teacher research seem limited unless one has the opportunity to undertake a Master's programme. Student teachers on Postgraduate Certificate in Education (PGCE) courses that attract Master's-level (M-level) credits have the considerable advantage of protected time to reflect critically on their work, to start to 'think research' and to begin to engage in research as they develop their teacher–researcher identities. The time spent in the classroom is, of course, invaluable for the many try-outs and to hone practical skills, but equally valuable is the time spent out of the classroom on a training course. This time-out provides a rich terrain for critical reflection, standing back, questioning, sharing, evaluating and thinking about different ways to do things. This is often where fruitful research activity begins.

The student teachers and teachers who feature in this chapter either work, or have worked, in urban contexts, and all have worked in London at some point. While most of the issues are relevant to all modern foreign languages (MFL) teachers in nearly every context, they are arguably of particular relevance in urban settings and especially in London where so many of the contested, researchable issues are greatly intensified in the hugely varied settings of urban schools.

Important though such reflective activity is for all trainee teachers, there is a particularly strong need for MFL teachers to begin early because there is a dearth of small-scale (and indeed larger-scale) research in the field of MFL compared to some other subjects. In fact, there are a great many accounts of small-scale research projects undertaken by MFL student teachers and teachers, but these often remain hidden, unshared and unpublished.

There are likely thousands of such projects in London training institutions alone if we consider the waves of trainees who have produced M-level assignments over the last few years, and it would be valuable to bring these to light. Raising awareness of the wealth of 'hidden' research would strengthen the status of MFL (under continuing attack in many quarters as regards its status as a legitimate curriculum subject for all learners), legitimate many practices that have been developed, subject some contested practices to critical scrutiny and create a greater sense of community in MFL research.

Toward an understanding of 'research'

In this chapter I explore the experiences of student teachers and some recently qualified teachers (RQTs) at varying stages in the process of developing their professional identity as teacher–researchers, to make sense of the dynamics and inconsistencies in their classroom life. The teachers whose work features in this chapter have undertaken classroom research stemming from questions arising from their classroom realities. Wilson (2013: 4) writes about the importance of the context of learning, emphasizing that: 'Professional learning and teacher knowledge is embodied, contextual and embedded in practice.' She also differentiates between different levels of 'conscious awareness':

> In day-to-day classroom interactions, teachers draw on their intuitive tacit knowledge gained through previous experience. This 'hot action' is coloured by feelings and reactions and relies on an instant response, building up 'knowledge in action'. More measured reactive or reflective learning takes place through interpretation of the situations accompanied by short reactive reflection which might take place at the end of a teaching episode or in conversation with another teacher.
>
> (Wilson, 2013: 4)

In this chapter, I understand the research process to embrace both this intuitive 'hot action' and 'short reactive reflection', and draw on the definition of research as 'systematic self-critical inquiry' (Stenhouse, 1981: 103), which has the following features:

- It constitutes pedagogic research and is undertaken **by** teachers, often **with** other teachers, not *on* teachers.
- It is driven by personal interest and a felt need.
- The pupil voice figures large in these investigations.
- Research is a natural extension of reflective practice.

Student teachers do not always start out with much previous experience, but gain experience exponentially throughout their training. The students are required to be critically reflective, and typically develop their reflexivity on Wilson's continuum as a matter of course and as they learn research skills.

Reflective practice and teacher research: Challenging the status quo

Teachers are no strangers to data. They are generators, collectors and receivers of a substantial volume of data in their daily practices, as Brighouse and Woods write: 'Teachers are natural researchers in the sense that all teaching is based on inquiry and the response of pupils provides ready evidence as to the effectiveness of various teaching and learning approaches' (Brighouse and Woods, 1999: 42). Teacher research is far from being new (Elliott, 1991; Stenhouse, 1975) and teachers have engaged in curriculum development-type activities with experienced researchers for many years. However, there is a key difference with regard to the modern concept of the teacher–researcher that emphasizes the agency of teachers in initiating and leading their own research. Indeed, Carr and Kemmis (1986) suggest that such research is emancipatory when it leads to teachers interrogating knowledge and challenging assumptions they might make about their practice. While teaching experience provides a rich frame of reference of what has worked (often anecdotal and potentially unchallenged), student teachers bring fresh eyes and relatively unprejudiced views, and often ask questions that can lead to better and different practices that challenge the status quo. They thus serve the purpose of helping to unsettle comfortable routines and counter the construct of fixed mindsets with those that can be 'grown' (Dweck, 2000).

A desire to research often springs from a sense of dissatisfaction, a felt need or self-questioning, or as Cochran-Smith and Lytle put it: 'Teachers' questions often emerge from discrepancies between what is intended and what occurs' (Cochran-Smith and Lytle, 1993: 14). This reflects perfectly the lived experience of student or new teachers, who go through considerable unsettledness, especially in the early days. These teachers find themselves in a quandary, for example, about target language (TL) use, independent pupil talk, peer- and self- assessment or the most effective learning strategies. The student teacher's natural response is to seek a better understanding of the phenomena they encounter, research possible solutions and find some equilibrium, as Cochran-Smith and Lytle suggest: 'Teacher research stems from or generates questions and reflects teachers' desires to make sense of their experience—to adapt a learning stance or openness toward classroom life' (ibid.: 25).

Teachers have long been considered reflective practitioners (Schön, 1987), but the development of the actively engaged teacher–researcher persona seems to be proposing a changed teacher mindset, from one that involves a largely reactive evaluation of practice to one that critically interrogates and re-evaluates personal pedagogical spaces. Larrivee suggests that critical reflexivity is the distinguishing feature of reflective practitioners as this reflexivity gives teachers 'the necessary sense of self-efficacy to create personal solutions to problems' (Larrivee, 2000: 294).

Some experienced teachers are scathing of what they perceive as research as something distant and unconnected to real-life classrooms and, as a result, their attitude leads to their self-exclusion from the research process. Arguing for a more proactive stance on the part of teachers, Burke and Kirton place teachers undertaking small-scale research 'at the centre of knowledge production in the professional context of the classroom', on the grounds that reflexivity 'helps to illuminate their own positions in educational processes'. Student teachers have, as yet, little such wariness and are willing and excited to start researching as part of their emerging professional identities, in their oft-expressed desire to 'make a difference' (Burke and Kirton, 2006: 1).

Transforming practice: A conceptual framing of the development of teacher–researchers

A prime consideration is the impact of the research on each teacher and their practice, in terms of potential transformation. Kennedy (2005) proposed a scale classifying organized activities in formal learning contexts (which in the case of these teachers is the PGCE with M-level credits). At the lowest level on the scale is the *transmissive* level, where teachers receive information from tutors, mentors, peers and self-study. The next level is the *translational* level, where teachers try out ideas and activities in their classrooms and learn (through trial and error) strategies that work well and that support learning, while becoming aware of the constraints of such strategies. At the *transformational* level, teachers undertake conscious reflection and start to analyse and evaluate their practice to understand and resolve tensions.

Kennedy's levels are helpful in reflecting on teachers' achievement of their aims as researchers. The teachers in this chapter had already experienced substantial transmission of knowledge at some recent stage in the training course, and varying experiences at the translational level at different stages of their career. The opportunity for structured research on the PGCE, with training in research methodologies and skills, enabled a potential shift to the next level, transformational activity. Wilson (op. cit.: 4), in a similar vein, suggests that change in practice results from 'deliberative learning' and a 'conscious management of thought and activity through setting aside time to learn'. The degree to which change occurs can be evaluated using Kennedy's framework in reflecting on the investigations carried out by teachers as emergent researchers, a process that begins in the initial training stage.

Student teachers: Acquiring research skills

The training period provides opportunities to develop basic pedagogic competences and skills, but it is also the ideal terrain for teachers to take a longer-term view on how they would like to develop their critical researcher personae. As part of this learning, students begin to understand how professional development is not separate from, but rather central to, effective teaching. Student teachers bring a certain mindset or 'fixed pattern of beliefs' (Tillema, 1997: 209) to their training, based on their own life experiences, but they are simultaneously opened to a shift in mindset if given the right learning conditions to promote this. Thus, there is an openness to consider alternative ways of doing things, an openness to do try-outs (within reason) and to query the status quo. Students are, in many ways, 'close' to the pupils and seemingly unafraid – indeed very keen – to consult them. Crucially, student teachers are given the time to undertake this critical reflection during their training.

The fact that PGCE training attracts M-level credit is very much in support of the research stance, since M-level research-focused investigations are required as part of the course. These give opportunities for trainees to engage with the research culture of the university. Each training partnership will have its own arrangements and induction into research. At King's College London (KCL), research is prioritized and carefully aligned with the teacher training programme. The KCL course requires trainees to undertake two small-scale research assignments (one a critical reflection on teaching and the progression of pupil learning, the other a critical exploration of practice in the light of policy), and to engage in, and investigate, classroom practice through a research lens. This involves exploring practices, observing in a systematic way, using research tools such as questionnaires and interviews and analysing a range of data collected throughout the course. KCL MFL student teachers also have opportunities to engage in research projects with other European Union countries. These have included, for example, the development and comparison of formative assessment in nine partner countries, and a comparison of pupil talk in post-16 classes in England and France. This is where the foreign language expertise of the student teachers is invaluably advantageous in allowing discussion and analysis to take place in a variety of languages, rather than project participants having to rely on the assumption of 'all speaking English' and on translation.

The student teachers' research is concurrent with their roles as trainees fully engaged on a PGCE course. They have support to ensure effective research planning, implementation, evaluation and ethical awareness. Experienced researchers provide training in the basic techniques of interviewing, focus groups and observation, and in text analysis to enable the students to critically appraise the many policy documents that, to some extent, frame their professional lives. The student teachers undertake both their own small-scale research projects and also research collaboratively, as the following examples demonstrate.

Student teachers' research projects: Some reflections
Some of the MFL research projects that student teachers have undertaken, and questions arising from the research in the academic year 2014/15, include:

1. *Primary–secondary transition*

In this project, the transition processes in a state primary and linked secondary were compared with those of an independent preparatory and its senior school. Both teachers and pupils were interviewed. The work found that the state Year 6 school pupils, notwithstanding some normal nervousness, keenly anticipated going to a new school and regarded the new learning in MFL exciting. The children in the independent school found just 'more of the same' and quickly became bored. Questions arose in the researcher's mind that challenged the assumptions embedded in the continuity–discontinuity dichotomy and fuelled the argument for what the researcher called more 'fresh learning' in terms of new content.

2. *Data*

As part of this project, teachers in one MFL department and a member of the senior leadership team (SLT) shared some of the official assessment data and were interviewed about how they interpreted and used them. The research found that, in spite of school policy directives, each teacher had his or her own take on the data and used them quite independently for their own purposes, with one teacher tracking pupils systematically, another using the data as a mere indicator of ability and another ignoring the data and creating his own pupil profiles.

Here the researcher began to question the status and usefulness, indeed the validity, of data and explore pupil equity considerations in a context of such contested and individualized use of data.

3. *Error*

This project was based on pupils in Year 10 attempting to identify errors in their own and a peer's written tasks, and to consider on what basis the errors might have been made. Their work was conducted over a period of a month, on four occasions. This intervention went beyond regular peer assessment toward a rich dialogue between pupils about how errors are made, carefully scaffolded by the teachers. The pupils identified what they considered to be unhelpful aspects of teaching that led to, for example, unfamiliarity with structures, misconceptions, a lack of time to think and what they perceived as the 'sheer illogicality of the foreign language'.

MFL teachers have long been fascinated by error. The imaginative feature of this research was that it asked pupils to attempt their own error analysis with peers (aided, of course, by teacher support) and encouraged them to say what it was about the teaching that might have caused error-making. Pupils are often asked about their learning but rarely about the teaching. Likewise, their errors are pointed-out by teachers but are rarely discussed.

4. Assessment for learning

It is known that assessment for learning (AfL) is interpreted differently in different subjects (Hodgen and Marshall, 2005). This study explored this issue in the MFL context, and was based on lesson observation of experienced teachers and interviews with teachers and pupils. AfL was found to be less dialogic in MFL teaching than in two other subjects, and more concerned with the 'twiddly bits' such as lolly sticks (bearing the pupils' names for random selection for questioning purposes) and traffic lighting (green, amber and red cards to indicate the level of pupils' understanding). Interestingly, in focus group discussions, Year 9 pupils showed an awareness of how their teachers interpreted AfL in their different subjects, and considered MFL practice 'routiney'. While subject variation in the use of AfL is fairly well known, this variation is not often acknowledged in school assessment policies nor discussed critically by MFL teachers. That the pupils found AfL rather 'routiney' would indicate a need for discussion about this by MFL teachers, since even what might be considered the best new practices can soon become boring, meaningless routines.

In conclusion to this section, it seems to me that, as well as providing insightful and fascinating findings for the student researchers at Kennedy's translational level in practice, there are findings here worthy of discussion in the larger MFL community. I move now to two examples of larger-scale research by RQTs, representing very different approaches.

Research by an RQT (Tulsi): 'How do you say 11 in Spanish?'

Following her PGCE, this RQT started research as part of her MA on an issue of real concern to her. Tulsi is a teacher of Spanish and French in a boys' comprehensive school in North London. Her research was inspired by the small-scale project she had undertaken on the PGCE and by an observation she found startling, a short time into her teaching career:

> I felt that, more often than not, generally in languages classrooms, teachers talk more than the pupils and that pupil-with-pupil talk is inadequate. I did one of my PGCE assignments on this. My MA research had a particular focus on speaking skills with the aim of understanding how to achieve more spontaneous target language [TL] from pupils during language lessons. In particular, I wanted to see how speaking skills, especially pupil-to-pupil,

could be encouraged with Year 8 classes, my own class and those of my colleagues.

Tulsi undertook her research over six weeks, embedding it into regular lessons, and was keen to engage her peers and pupils in the research:

> I wanted to involve my colleagues in this research and also hear and give value to the pupil voice. I observed colleagues' lessons, then interviewed them. I also held a focus group of eight students from each class observed, who were openly invited to give their opinions and ideas on their learning with an emphasis on speaking skills, to gain insights into the ways they considered speaking skills were developed and valued in their lessons.

Regarding the findings, Tulsi observed:

> I found a considerable amount of TL used in the case of the teachers but not quite enough on the part of the students. The teachers thought they themselves used more TL than they did. The pupils thought they needed and would have liked to use much more. Even when asking for a translation or how to say a particular word in Spanish, they are asking one another in English things like:
>
> Pupil A: Hey how do you say 11 again?
> Pupil B: Once [pupil says the number 11 in Spanish].
> Pupil A: Thanks, I forgot.
>
> I concluded that there was a need for the creation of more opportunities for TL to be used not only between teacher and student but among students themselves. Preparing for exams rather than the learning of a language in a communicative way is seen as a hindrance to more spontaneous speaking. Even small changes with regards to the promotion of and exposure to speaking skills such as encouraging more spontaneous answers to questions rather than set responses which have been memorized and more collaborative pupil working have the potential to give speaking skills more of a central role in the MFL classroom.

As regards the impact and actions resulting from the research, Tulsi noted:

> The changes I have made to my teaching since my research are noticeable. I have adopted the 'TL lifestyle' – using the TL by

default as Christie [2013] argues – with many of my groups, encouraging them to join in and feel immersed in language learning. My colleagues have also put this practice into place and have seen already, in the first half of this term, some positive outcomes. With the adopted changes, the students in my school are slowly but surely finding the increased use of TL by not only the teacher but themselves, a normal habit during the lessons. I think this is something other teachers could do, both the research and the focus on more pupil TL speaking.

In her PGCE research assignment, Tulsi had asserted that using the TL was time-consuming, not always justifiable and arguably ineffective. Yet that early research sowed seeds of doubt as she saw that her pupils did not actually talk to each very much in the TL. As a result, she revisited the topic on a bigger scale in this qualitative study, obtaining a wider range of data over a half term in normal timetabled lessons. She changed her views, from initial scepticism to the adoption of a new 'lifestyle' in the classroom. She invited her colleagues' involvement in co-researching. She also listened attentively to pupils who influenced her thinking. She has, I suggest, transformed both her mindset and her practice and has begun to have an impact on practice in classrooms beyond her own. Change happens not through mandate or directive, but through the encouragement of individual teacher practices and the engagement of teachers at classroom level.

Research by an RQT (Nicola): Putting a spanner in the works

Nicola, who teaches German and French in a mixed comprehensive in a town just outside of London, also caught the research habit from her PGCE days and remains an inquisitive and critical thinker about her practice. This has led to her undertaking a series of small-scale classroom research projects during her early years in teaching, such as exploring ways to empower learners with special educational needs in the languages classroom, developing challenge for more able pupils and promoting peer assessment. Her latest research has focused on how to extend speaking skills:

> The study group comprised a group of more able pupils who are on the gifted and talented register for MFL (a mixture of boys and girls, aged 12–13). I have always been far more interested in the acquisition and application of oral/aural skills in the target language than the written word. While many colleagues would argue a succinct essay is the ideal way of demonstrating

proficiency in the target language, my argument as a non-native is to be able to communicate what I need orally and to get what I need accomplished. Obviously at Key Stage 3, the scenarios are limited due to their age, but they would still need to be able to express their desires/needs in a monolingual TL situation.

Using a directed learning focus, I wanted to see if role playing helps students to independently use language in different, non-teacher directed ways. As an MFL teacher I have found students begin Year 7 with great enthusiasm and desire to 'have a go!' and just communicate – they seem to know no fear. As soon as they have sat their first written assessment, accuracy becomes their all-encompassing focus. Students lose their willingness to try. This might be explained by hormones and peer pressure, but it is, in my opinion, an indicator that we need to give students time and space to just speak without the pressure of the pass/fail exam.

Here, Nicola explains how she came to want to investigate and improve what she considered to be an unsatisfactory situation regarding pupils' speaking skills. She also expresses her belief about what she thinks MFL learning is for – for unrehearsed, spontaneous speech. She elaborated on how she conducted her piece of small-scale action research:

The initial topic was Year 8 healthy living – visiting the doctor. This topic, I feel, is important as it is something pupils might come across should they ever visit Germany, and it is in precisely this situation they would need to come up with new phrases to suit their need. I created mixed ability and gender groups. The intervention was as follows:

- I had an initial role play task (speaking assessment) in which I gauged their ability to adapt, change and (eventually?) create their own language using patterns we have learned as a whole class.
- They were given three one-hour sessions (and one homework session) to write notes, practice and rehearse with props for their performance. I gave the pupils a 'basics book', or *Mappe*, to remind them of the language we had learnt for this topic.
- The group were then told their role play must include an argument or being unable to pay due to lack of insurance or some such 'spanner in the works'. I offered moral support, but not language-based support.

- Prior to the lesson three students had been set homework to prepare their doctor role plays. They then performed them in this lesson.
- After this topic, I marked their efforts, made notes of phrases used outside of the *Mappe* and then completed this again with the next topic (going out/declining invitations to go out). This research took one full school term; half a term per topic.

Throughout lesson two, I offered 'hover-support'. Students would ask me questions relating to the language of the *Mappe*, pronunciation, which word could be changed (a perfectly standard question in my classroom) and so on, as I 'hovered' around. Students were reminded to have fun with it.

Looking back on the experience, Nicola reflected:

The target group were asked to try and include some phrases beyond the scope of the original brief, for example, an accident 'en route', and dealt well with this challenge. Students were able to adapt accurately phrases provided in the *Mappe* to change costs, reasons for not being able to pay, questioning the doctor's decisions or providing interruptions with different characters (e.g. children), using work we had done previously on grammar. The pupils spoke confidently and were able to use adapted phrases in their later year exam.

She found that pupils enjoyed the performances and working as a team: 'checking everyone knows their lines and does the right thing at the right time'. The pupils identified a number of benefits to this approach, referring in their feedback to: 'helping us to string together longer sentences'; 'I feel a lot more confident to just try and talk in German'; and 'There's a lot more topics we can speak about in German now'.

In terms of impact, Nicola felt her practice had changed as a direct result of her action research and its positive outcomes:

This has already impacted my practice. I have found resources to get my students to maintain and practise their knowledge of justifications and gut reactions. I ask some higher-order thinking questions in the target language as students can refer to their sentence starters and use their *Mappe* for help. These are all the kinds of tasks MFL teachers do already but [they] can tweak their practice slightly, for example by giving only sentence starters or phrases with gaps. The key areas for other MFL teachers are to:

1 – maintain [their] own 'have a go' attitude – it can be easy to fall back into comfortable habits when teaching full lesson days
2 – challenge the students by not accepting their first answer, asking 'why?' and prompting them to give a more detailed answer
3 – assume that students can, when pushed, find the language required. You are slightly less indispensable than you previously thought!

As with Tulsi, Nicola considered that other teachers could easily tweak their practice to achieve similar results. In addition, pragmatically anticipating change (rather than waiting to be overwhelmed by impending change), she concluded that, given that new examination specifications would necessitate more pupil-to-pupil interactions, her proactive research interventions had provided her with a range of strategies that would prove useful in enabling such interactions.

Conclusion

The small-scale research undertaken and enjoyed by teachers discussed in this chapter testifies to the power of such modest investigations and to the teachers' developing self-agency. The teachers involved colleagues and/or the pupils, enabling more sustainable practice. Sustainability requires creative, reflexive and participative learning processes such as those described. Even small-scale actions taken by one teacher have the potential to influence way beyond the one teacher–one classroom context and create transformative practice.

Teachers like talking about their work, and doing research creates a shift, from what Hopkins and Lagerweij refer to as the 'anecdotal evidence and perceptual data collected unsystematically' by teachers (1996: 88) to the posing of important questions that can seed a more systematic type of teacher-research of wider value. Crucially, the teacher–researchers in this chapter were encouraged to listen to pupil views (for this is not automatic on the part of teachers), with sometimes surprising results. Indeed, the learners have been given a more active role in their learning and a measure of self-agency, and their interests were at the heart of these research projects. Emphasizing the value of the student voice, Flutter and Rudduck write: 'Pupils of all ages can show a remarkable capacity to discuss their learning in a considered and insightful way … There is also evidence to suggest that it may also have a beneficial effect on pupils' performance' (Flutter and Rudduck, 2004: 7).

The accounts in this chapter demonstrate the agency of new teachers in pioneering small-scale research in MFL classrooms and staking a claim to this terrain as emergent researchers inhabiting this role as part of their evolving teacher identity. Burke and Kirton suggest that teacher research empowers teachers to have a voice in classroom-focused research and in their construction of knowledge from an insider position – a position 'of great value in developing more nuanced and complex understandings of educational experiences, identities, processes, practices and relations' (Burke and Kirton, 2006: 2).

Research in these terms is for the many, not the few. When teachers are given the time and space to become involved in a more participatory, collaborative kind of reflection involving peers as co-researchers, while listening to the student voice and engaging with theory, the results can be very powerful. From there, teacher–researchers can legitimately question existing agendas and begin to set their own, as Pring (2000) argues. In the highly contested and changeable fields of teaching, learning and assessment in languages, such questioning from trainee and new teachers is to be welcomed and encouraged, as is the active search for responses to those questions.

Implications for future practice

There are many implications (for MFL teachers, schools and those working in the field of MFL teacher education) arising from the narratives and reflections in this chapter. These include the need to:

- reframe the theory–practice divide as an integral and essential whole in the field of MFL pedagogic practice. The divide is false and unnecessary. It is essential that teachers have a solid rationale and justification for what they do in practice and be able to explain and give valid accounts of why they think practice is effective, or indeed ineffective. These explanations and accounts involve theorizing precepts and relating practice to theories of learning rather than just giving opinions relating to their own contexts.
- re-assert the value of the unique contribution of university culture and expertise in research in MFL teacher training and teacher education. Teacher training is a partnership between the university setting and the schools' contexts, and always has been. Respecting the expertise of each domain and making practical arrangements in the training

for rich cross-referencing of such expertise lay the foundations for teachers to become critically reflective practitioners.

- re-define the university–school training partnership as a basis for joint investigation into MFL pedagogic practices. The partnership need not restrict itself to the objective of student teachers meeting a set of rather 'technical' standards, but might re-conceptualize the training vision to include exploratory inquiry into practice for the benefit of – and inclusion of – both training partners.
- enrich the MFL field by encouraging small-scale research that involves teachers and is designed to 'unsettle' and question the status quo. Such research is, as argued in this chapter, ideally initiated in the early teacher training stage so that teachers enter the profession with some research skills and experience, and the desire to continue to practice research as a matter of course.
- include small-scale, personalized and contextualized research as part of whole-school continuing professional development (CPD), by validating research as valuable and relevant teacher learning and by giving teachers the necessary time and space to research issues of interest to them.
- ensure the support of leadership for such initiatives in the development of MFL good practice. MFL practice flourishes where senior leadership gives it a high priority and champions the MFL cause. Finding ways to disseminate and share research findings in and beyond the local school community would add immeasurably both to the MFL profile in schools and also to the national picture.
- facilitate networks of MFL teachers to share and validate the findings of such research. Currently much small-scale research remains unshared or available only to special interest groups, subscription-only journals or conference-goers.

In conclusion, support is needed to enable teachers to engage with research in a more accessible and democratic way.

Questions for practice

Questions that MFL students and new and more experienced teachers might ask:

- What happens in your classroom that you find you are dissatisfied with and that you think could be improved/done differently/transformed?
- How could you usefully engage the pupils in reflecting on these concerns and giving feedback on what is helpful to their learning?

- How could you collaborate with or engage your colleagues in your research?

Further reading

Flutter, J. and Rudduck, J. (2004) *Consulting Pupils: What's in it for schools?* London: RoutledgeFalmer.

Wallace, M.J. (1997) *Action Research for Language Teachers.* Cambridge: CUP.

Wilson, E. (2013) *School-Based Research: A guide for education students.* Cambridge: CUP.

References

Brighouse, T. and Woods, P. (1999) *How to Improve Your School.* London: Methuen.

Bryant, I. (1996) 'Action research and reflective practice'. In Scott, D. and Usher, R. (eds), *Understanding Educational Research.* London: Routledge.

Burke, P.J. and Kirton, A. (2006) 'The insider perspective: Teachers-as-researchers'. *Reflecting Education*, 2 (1), 1–4.

Carr, W. and Kemmis, S. (1986) *Becoming Critical Educators: Knowledge and action research.* London: RoutledgeFalmer.

Christie, C. (2013) 'Speaking spontaneously in the modern foreign languages classroom: Tools for supporting successful target language conversation'. *Language Learning Journal*, October, 1–16. Online. www.tandfonline.com/doi/abs/10.1080/09571736.2013.836751 (accessed 3 July 2016).

Cochran-Smith, M. and Lytle, S. (1993) *Inside Outside: Teacher research and knowledge.* New York: Teachers College Press.

Dweck, C. (2000) *Self-Theories: Their role in motivation, personality, and development.* New York: Psychology Press.

Elliott, J. (1991) *Action Research for Educational Change.* Buckingham: Open University Press.

Flutter, J. and Rudduck, J. (2004) *Consulting Pupils: What's in it for schools?* London: RoutledgeFalmer.

Hodgen, J. and Marshall, B. (2005) 'Assessment for learning in English and mathematics: A comparison'. *The Curriculum Journal*, 16 (2), 153–76.

Hopkins, D. and Lagerweij, N. (1996). 'The school improvement knowledge base'. In Reynolds, D., Bollen, R., Creemers, B., Hopkins, D., Stoll, L. and Lagerweij, N. (eds), *Making Good Schools: Linking school effectiveness and school improvement.* London: Routledge.

Kennedy, A. (2005) 'Models of continuing professional development: A framework for analysis'. *Journal of In-Service Education*, 32 (2), 235–50.

Kincheloe, J. (2003) *Teachers as Researchers: Qualitative inquiry as a path to empowerment.* London: RoutledgeFalmer.

Lane, S., Lacefield-Parachini, N. and Isken, J. (2003) 'Developing novice teachers as change agents'. *Teacher Education Quarterly*, Spring, 55–68.

Larrivee, B. (2000) 'Transforming teaching practice: Becoming the critically reflective teacher'. *Reflective Practice*, 1 (3), 293–307.

Pring, R. (2000) *Philosophy of Education Research.* London: Continuum.

Schön, D. (1987) *The Reflective Practitioner*. London: Arena.

Stenhouse, L. (1975) *An Introduction to Curriculum Research and Development*. London: Heinemann.

— (1981) 'What counts as research?' *British Journal of Educational Studies*, 29 (2), 103–14.

Tillema, H.H. (1997) 'Stability and change in student teacher beliefs'. *European Journal of Teacher Education*, 20 (3), 209–12.

Toffler, A. (1970) *Future Shock*. New York: Bantam Books.

Wilson, E. (2013) *School-Based Research: A guide for education students*. Cambridge: CUP.

Chapter 2

Creating and nurturing resilient MFL teams

Anna Lise Gordon

Resilience: More than just another buzzword?

A recent government announcement focused on the importance of developing 'resilient' pupils with the 'grit' needed to succeed in modern Britain (DfE, 2014). Indeed, the current resurgence of interest in Dweck's (2006) notion of a growth mindset in many schools may be linked to this new initiative. While it is undoubtedly important to nurture pupils' resilience, this chapter focuses specifically on the resilience of modern foreign languages (MFL) teachers working together, in positive, proactive teams, to enhance pupils' learning.

Currently, there is considerable interest in teacher resilience in general terms, ranging from research-informed articles (such as Gu and Day, 2013) to practical guidance for teachers on managing their own professional well-being (such as Holmes, 2005). This interest is further emphasized by the seemingly constant media focus on teacher stress, exemplified by a recent independent survey of teachers' levels of job satisfaction and well-being (Communicate Research Ltd, 2013). This survey indicated that 47 per cent of respondents had seriously considered leaving the profession, while 86 per cent commented that their workload had increased in the previous year. Although these are general figures, it is likely that these findings resonate with MFL teams, too.

Specific reference to initial teacher education (ITE) in the work of MFL teams will be made later in this chapter, but it is worth noting that resilience has been a key focus in recent documentation around entry to the teaching profession in particular (DfE, 2011; Carter, 2015). The Carter review stresses the importance of nurturing the resilience of new teachers and encourages those involved in initial teacher training to emphasize to new teachers that they are joining one of the most valued professions, as this will be 'an important motivating force that can build resilience and pride in new teachers, helping to sustain them in the first few challenging years of their career' (Carter, 2015: 25). Unfortunately, no mention is made of resilience in the summary of recommendations, so it is perhaps unsurprising that nurturing resilience of early career teachers does not feature in the government's response (DfE, 2015) to Carter's review.

Against this general contextual background, even just a short time spent reading the Association for Language Learning (ALL) website or following #mfltwitterati on Twitter will highlight some of the more specific and current challenges to the resilience for MFL teams. Many of the teachers mentioned in the case studies later in this chapter cite the importance of being a member of MFL networks as a way of keeping abreast of new developments, learning from publications and regular updates, exploring new initiatives and accessing professional development activities and resources. As one teacher commented: 'Attending ALL events is vital; they give me an injection of enthusiasm and renewed energy in challenging times!'

As an ITE tutor, I am often asked by MFL teachers how other schools are dealing with particular issues. Some of the issues they have raised over the last year have included:

- ways of encouraging more pupils to continue MFL study in key stage 4 (KS4)
- concerns about teacher recruitment
- requests for guidance on the KS2–KS3 transition
- support for curriculum developments, including approaches to translation and literary texts
- the new GCSE and A-level examination requirements
- integration of new technology applications, especially iPads
- research evidence and suggested reading on particular issues, such as promoting spontaneous use of target language (TL) and motivation
- focus on developing independent writing and grammar in schemes of work
- planning for assessment without National Curriculum (NC) levels
- raising the profile of MFL, including working with foreign language assistants and school trips.

A resilient team, faced with constant change in the system, needs to plan ahead to meet the needs of its own context, and this links closely with the importance of research-informed practice, as outlined in the opening chapter of this book. For example, as one head of department (HoD) commented: 'Having identified changes in the GCSE speaking exam, and the inclusion of translations in the writing exam, we have adapted our KS3 assessments, increasing the pupils' familiarity with the format along with the staff.'

As a teacher educator, I have the privilege of working with some outstanding MFL teams who, in different ways, play their part in nurturing the resilience of MFL teachers and learners. This might include developing a colleague's linguistic subject knowledge for teaching a second language in KS3 or supporting a colleague with strategies for managing behaviour in pair- and group-work speaking activities. It might include whole-team foci, such as preparing pupils for the new GCSE requirements, re-writing a scheme of work to develop pupils' spontaneous TL use or making effective use of iPads in the MFL classroom. The list is endless, but being part of a resilient MFL team is beneficial in all situations. The next section of this chapter looks at what it means to be resilient, both personally and professionally.

MFL teams and resilience

What is resilience? And what is resilience when viewed through the lens of the MFL team? Is it more than 'coping with life's little wobbles', as noted in a headline in the *Times Educational Supplement* (Bloom, 2013: 14)? Neenan (2009: 3) describes resilience as an 'intriguing yet elusive concept', but just a brief glance at translations of the word 'resilience' in languages commonly taught in many UK schools gives an indication of its meaning: *Elastizität, résistance, resistencia, elasticità, resiliens ...*

Potential Teach First applicants learn that when 'faced with obstacles, you will need to be tenacious and versatile and maintain a positive mindset' (Teach First: online). While one may debate whether such a statement is an attractive view of teaching and why such qualities are particularly required by teachers, few would argue that resilience is needed in the profession. Much of the literature around resilience refers to the importance of being able to 'bounce back' from difficulties or setbacks. Every MFL team will be able to think of occasions when there is a need to bounce back from setbacks, such as a disappointing set of examination results, retirement of an experienced and valued colleague or lack of interest in a planned trip abroad. Schools can be pressurized environments with a wide range of competing demands, so there is a need for strong MFL teachers who are self-aware and able to reflect on their own individual needs, as well as the needs of their subject and pastoral teams. However, the good news is that the combination of personality and experience within a team means that the building blocks are in place for ongoing development. Based on their research, Gu and Day (2013: 22) are confident that 'conditions count' with regard to nurturing teacher resilience, and I would argue that ensuring that the conditions are right is a shared responsibility of everyone in an

MFL team. There is no quick-fix toolkit approach to developing a resilient team; a well-considered, open and reflective style of working together for the benefit of teachers and learners over the longer term is required.

It is worth considering two descriptions of resilience when reflecting on what it means to be a resilient MFL team. Both references are general, but can be easily applied to the MFL team context. The first description is taken from the work of Robertson Cooper, an organization that focuses on resilience and well-being in the workplace. Although its work does not specifically refer to educational contexts, the free online *i-resilience* test (available at www.robertsoncooper.com) is useful for any individual or team wishing to explore its resilience in more detail. Trainee teachers at St Mary's University are encouraged to complete this test to generate a personalized report providing an overview of the individual's resilience and, importantly, guidance and a suggested action plan for future development. The Robertson Cooper approach suggests that a good starting point for individuals, leaders and teams is to focus on four key aspects that we draw on for our resilience: confidence, adaptability, purposefulness and the need for social support. These four aspects link closely with Gu and Day's description (2013: 26) of teacher resilience as 'the capacity to maintain equilibrium and a sense of commitment and agency in the everyday worlds in which teachers teach'.

With this in mind, a resilient MFL team needs to be confident and able to adapt; it will have a shared sense of purpose and be mutually supportive. A couple of real-life examples from MFL teams serve to illustrate the point (some details have been adapted to retain confidentiality):

- Despite strong and well-considered arguments to the contrary from the MFL team, the senior management team has decided to phase out German and replace it with Spanish in the MFL curriculum. For many teachers, this is a challenge to their confidence and their adaptability. Although the core values of the team have been maintained, as pupils will continue to have the opportunity to learn two languages, there is clearly a need for adaptability and social support at this time of transition. Perhaps one teacher will actively seek a position with German in another school? Perhaps some of the team will accept the school's offer of significant continuous professional development (CPD) funding to learn Spanish together? Perhaps German will be offered as a popular option in the school's enrichment provision? There are many other possible options in this scenario, but they all require resilience and the ability to respond positively to a difficult situation.

- It is mid-August and the MFL team is faced with worse GCSE examination results than expected. Although broadly supportive of the MFL team, the senior leadership team (SLT) has demanded a response and action plan. This is clearly a challenge to the confidence of the MFL team, which needs to work together to consider complex issues, including differences in results between languages, teachers and groups of pupils. Although a data-driven analysis is needed, the emotional aspect of the situation must not be underestimated. Boud *et al.* are clear on this point: 'The affective dimension has to be taken into account when we are engaged in our own learning activities, and when we are assisting others in this process' (Boud *et al.*, 1985: 11). A measured approach, over time, is likely to sustain resilience most effectively. As Hargreaves and Fink note: 'Change in education is easy to propose, hard to implement, and even harder to sustain' (Hargreaves and Fink, 2007: 1). Perhaps specific intervention support for one teacher is needed? Perhaps the scheme of work needs to be revised to include a stronger focus on particular skills? Perhaps additional external CPD is needed, including collaboration with other local MFL teams? Again, there are many other possible options to nurture resilience for the team to ensure teacher and pupil well-being in the longer term.

I conclude this section with a challenging comment by Neenan: 'you don't develop resilience by staying in your comfort zone' (Neenan, 2009: 75). Rather than dwelling on a potentially disappointing or stressful situation, a resilient MFL team will manage the situation by adopting a more productive and purposeful approach. This is exemplified in the following short case studies from four MFL teams. The schools have worked in partnership with St Mary's University for a number of years, including engagement with ITE and CPD opportunities.

Case study 1: MFL team leader as a resilient learner

One of the distinguishing features of a resilient department is that the head of department (HoD) acts as a role model. This may be in relation to managing workload, embracing change, responding to challenges and so on. It may also relate to openness to learning and trying new approaches to MFL teaching and learning. As one such HoD, Marion, says: 'I try to be the buffer between the demands of the school and the teachers in my team. I see it as part of my role to take on the stress and pass it on only when necessary and in a minimized version.'

While working as HoD, Marion completed a part-time MA related to KS3 assessment, which was highly beneficial in terms of addressing a challenging issue in MFL for the department. Colleagues in the department refer to her zest for learning and for ensuring that curriculum innovation is evidence-based, combining more theoretical research with classroom practice. As part of her research project she sought feedback from pupils, using the learner's voice to inform developments. Approaching the conclusion of the MA research inquiry, she observes:

> This research project has been part of my life for over a year now and it has been a fascinating journey. Using something that I was interested in, but also that I needed to address due to current changes in education, made the project fully relevant. The question 'how to assess meaningfully at KS3 without using NC levels' is one that all secondary schools have been dealing with over the last two years and I like to think the framework I created as an answer provides a workable solution for French.

As a leader of an MFL team, responsibilities are varied and sometimes challenging, but ensuring a research-informed approach to a significant issue in this way, with the 'teacher as model learner' (Hammond, 2015: 59), ensures that a resilient department is able to approach changes with confidence.

Case study 2: Growing resilient teachers within the team

As an outstanding trainee teacher on placement, Syanne was delighted to be offered a newly qualified teacher (NQT) position in the same school. She is in no doubt that communication is central to the success of her resilient MFL team. The department meets regularly to discuss plans, and seeks advice when needed. The teachers share resources freely and observe one another regularly, especially when someone wants to trial a new idea and receive additional feedback. There is a clear sense of shared purpose in the team and a high level of professional support.

Some of Syanne's insights about her own workload as a trainee teacher and NQT are helpful in relation to her development as a resilient teacher:

> I remember struggling with my workload during my PGCE and I found myself working six weekends straight with no break. However, I was scared of speaking up as I thought this was normal. At this time, I realized how important communication was and [so I] spoke with my university tutor. I was surprised to

be set a target to take a day off at the weekend! I always remember that and have followed that advice during my NQT year.

The importance of open lines of communication has been further highlighted for Syanne as an NQT. As an enthusiastic teacher who is keen to seize all of the opportunities that come her way, she found that more and more was being added to her role. Although she was enthused by these opportunities, she reached a breaking point:

> I remember taking a step back and thinking about how I was going tell my HoD how I was feeling. I contacted my former university tutor and other teacher friends for advice. When I spoke to my her, I felt a sense of release and, since then, any new opportunities have been discussed fully in advance.

Syanne now has responsibility for KS3 and mentoring an NQT in the MFL team. She knows her good organization will be essential, but she has also learnt a lot about managing workload and taking care when delegating responsibilities. Syanne's story is an example of a resilient MFL team that recognizes strengths in new teachers and proactively grows its own future leaders.

Case study 3: Resilient teams collaborate with learners

The importance of positive relationships between teachers and learners is widely acknowledged. HoD Juliette has led a 'learner voice' initiative to guide developments in her MFL team (and in the wider school) over a number of years. The initiative is aimed at exploring students' perceptions of how they learn best and how teaching approaches could be enhanced to help them learn better. Juliette comments that the initiative needs reviewing each year as 'each generation changes and responds differently to technologies, games, translation activities, reading in the target language etc.' Alongside student surveys, sixth form linguists conduct interviews with a sample of students across year groups and languages, including focus groups for bilingual students and Pupil Premium students, among others.

In one year of the Learner Voice initiative, a number of areas were identified for MFL. With regard to the quality of teaching, the pupils in lower KS3 requested more games and interactive tasks, whereas Year 9 pupils requested a greater focus on GCSE-style activities during the year. Pupils were also keen to have a stronger focus on strategies for learning vocabulary and grammar. As a result of the initiative, significant changes were introduced to the MFL approach to assessment for learning. Rather than the 'what went well (www)/even better if (ebi)' approach, this was changed to www/action (challenge) in feedback from teachers, and pupils requested that more time be allowed in class to respond to feedback and ask questions as needed.

From the resilience perspective, the benefits of this approach are significant for both teachers and learners. The level of mutual understanding ensures better student–teacher relationships, while better dialogue about learning ensures that teachers are able to plan more effectively. The openness of teachers to respond to feedback via the Learner Voice initiative also serves as a good role model for learners.

Case study 4: Continual support for team resilience

After a long period of stability, changes in staffing over the last two years have meant that Ruth has had to reflect on how to nurture and sustain resilience in her evolving MFL team.

As an experienced HoD, Ruth has a range of useful strategies to enhance resilience of new colleagues, such as planning departmental meetings across the year to focus on key issues in a timely manner, highlighting potential pressure points well in advance, regular one-to-one meetings to discuss any concerns and reassuring and encouraging colleagues in their work. When asked how she supports the resilience of her team, Ruth is honest:

> Chocolate at regular intervals ... A termly thank-you card and gift ... always including thanks and positives in team meetings ... encouraging new colleagues to share ideas and good practice ... finding ways to minimize and spread the workload ... sometimes downplaying the stressfulness of a busy period.

Many MFL team leaders would find staffing changes challenging, but Ruth tries to approach the situation with a positive attitude. As she approaches the new academic year with four new members in the team, all taking GCSE classes, and with Spanish in Year 10 for the first time, she will need to draw on her own personal and professional resilience. Like many resilient leaders, one way that Ruth achieves this is by keeping 'ahead of the game' and engaging with regular CPD opportunities, including small MFL events at a local level. In this way, she actively researches new ideas to be able to share them and grow the team as a result.

Implications for future practice

There are undoubtedly a number of recurring stresses in the teaching profession, including the demands of assessment and marking, constantly chasing pupils for homework, providing additional revision classes for

Year 11 pupils, meeting the needs of Pupil Premium learners and organizing trips abroad, to name but a few. However, positivity is tangible in the majority of MFL teams in the London area covered by this research, as teachers work together to inspire a future generation with an appreciation of languages. As one NQT said, 'I'd rather work hard in this job than any other job!'

Two suggestions for activities are now described, which arose from CPD sessions with MFL teams. They are intended as prompts for thinking space, which is so often lacking in busy MFL teams and school environments in general, and as an opportunity to 'reflect systematically' as required by the Teachers' Standards (DfE, 2012). Creating and nurturing a resilient team takes time and constant care, but the benefits of reflective practice are significant, both for individuals within the team and for the team as a whole.

Activity 1: Focus on resilience as a team
The four aspects of resilience mentioned earlier in this chapter – confidence, adaptability, purposefulness and the need for social support – provide a useful framework for team discussion on key issues. The four aspects can be revisited on a regular basis, with questions adapted for a different focus each time. The following example relates to a planned discussion about literature in the KS3 MFL curriculum:

Confidence: What literature are we already using in KS3? Do we use literature particularly well in certain units of the scheme of work and/or in certain languages? What different types of literature might we use?

Adaptability: How might we adapt a few units in the scheme of work to include some poetry or short stories? How will we make authentic texts accessible for our learners?

Purposefulness: Are we clear about how literature fits into the KS3 National Curriculum? What are the benefits and the challenges for us as a team? What resources do we have/need to support this aspect of the curriculum?

Social support: Who is particularly interested in literature in KS3 and might take a lead in this area? How can we draw on others for support? For example: the ALL literature wiki (http://all-literature.wikidot.com).

Activity 2: A 'diamond nine' of resilience challenges
Even the most resilient MFL teams will encounter periods of intensity, and this activity is useful to gauge the temperature of the team at a given moment in time. The responses serve as a useful basis for discussion of priorities and possible solutions.

Individuals identify up to nine challenges to their resilience as a teacher and member of the MFL team, noting each on a separate small piece of paper. These may range from major challenges (such as 'improve my subject knowledge for Year 10 French teaching') or medium challenges ('manage poor behaviour of Year 9 set 4 more effectively') to seemingly trivial challenges ('find time to buy birthday present for grandmother'). It is important that participants have free choice about what to note at this stage.

Once the challenges have been noted, individuals arrange them in a 'diamond nine' according to the level of intensity, with the biggest challenge to resilience at the top. They then share their responses with their colleagues (supported and facilitated by the HoD). Here is an example from one teacher:

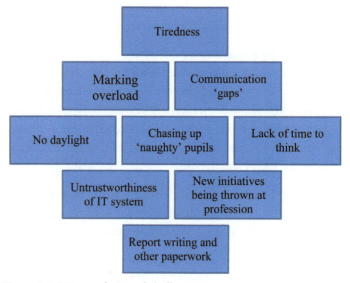

Figure 2.1: Diamond nine of challenges

The group's shared view of individual responses forms the basis for discussion and action, as appropriate. Clearly, some challenges are directly within the control of the MFL team, others will need to be addressed by the individual (such as tiredness), others need to be taken into the wider school context (for instance, the IT issue in this example) and others are much broader in scope (such as new initiatives being introduced). Regarding the specific context of Figure 2.1, the HoD was aware of the pressures of marking, but this challenge was highlighted so strongly by all members of the team in the 'diamond nine' activity that it led to a review of marking processes in MFL.

This can also be a useful activity on a smaller scale, for example for a mentor working with a stressed trainee teacher or a senior leader working with a HoD to identify team priorities.

And finally …

This chapter began with reference to MFL team involvement with ITE, as so many trainee teachers have commented over the years about the importance of a supportive mentor and a positive MFL team for developing and nurturing their resilience in the early stages of their professional trajectory.

Resilient MFL teams are often actively involved in ITE provision. This is partly as a result of their commitment to the future of the profession, but also as a way to ensure quality recruitment to the team. It is also based on a recognition that mutual learning, including breadth of experience, comes from collaboration with the ITE provider. As one HoD comments about ITE partnership, 'A strong trainee who contributes good ideas can energize the team and have a positive effect as a result.'

The strongest theme to emerge from discussion with trainee teachers is the importance of relationships. The best mentor–trainee teacher relationships are built on trust and include an appropriate level of challenge. They balance the steady acquisition of skills with appropriate risk-taking to encourage creativity. They also include a deliberate focus on careful reflection with time to learn from experiences and plan for future development. When these relationships are reflected across the MFL team as a whole, resilience will not be far away.

Questions for practice

- How do the issues highlighted as examples in this chapter resonate with you and your colleagues in your own particular context?
- What other issues have occupied your thinking and discussions recently?
- How might they be addressed? What would your case study look like?
- Why not try the *i-resilience* test on www.robertsoncooper.com? This is a good starting point for reflection on personal and professional resilience.

Further reading

Duggan, L. and Solomons, M. (2014) *Building Resilience.* Calne, Wiltshire: Developing Potential Group.
Robertson, D. (2012) *Build Your Resilience.* London: Hodder Education.
Zolli, A. and Healy, A. (2012) *Resilience.* London: Headline Publishing Group.

Acknowledgements

Thanks to MFL colleagues in the following schools – especially Marion, Syanne, Ruth and Juliette – for sharing their stories of resilient MFL teams:

Gumley House Convent School, Isleworth
St Mark's Catholic School, Hounslow
St Paul's Catholic College, Sunbury
The Heathland School, Hounslow

References

Bloom, A. (2013) 'Coping with life's little wobbles'. *TESpro*, 8 March, 14–15.

Boud, D., Keogh, R. and Walker, D. (1985) *Reflection: Turning experience into learning*. London: RoutledgeFalmer.

Carter, A. (2015) *Carter Review of Initial Teacher Training (ITT)*. London: Department for Education.

Communicate Research Ltd (2013) *Teachers' Satisfaction and Wellbeing in the Workplace*. London: Communicate Research Ltd.

Department for Education (2011) *Training Our Next Generation of Outstanding Teachers: Implementation plan*. London: Department for Education.

— (2012) *Teachers' Standards Effective from 1 September 2012*. London: Department for Education.

— (2014) 'Measures to help schools instil character in pupils announced'. Press release. Online. www.gov.uk/government/news/measures-to-help-schools-instil-character-in-pupils-announced (accessed 8 December 2014).

— (2015) *Government Response to the Carter Review of Initial Teacher Training (ITT)*. London: Department for Education.

Dweck, C. (2006) *Mindset: The new psychology of success*. New York: Random House Publishing.

Gu, Q. and Day, C. (2013) 'Challenges to teacher resilience: Conditions count'. *British Educational Research Journal*, 39 (1), 22–44.

Hammond, A. (2015) *Teaching for Character*. Woodbridge: John Catt Educational Ltd.

Hargreaves, A. and Fink, D. (2007) 'Energizing leadership for sustainability'. In Davies, B. (ed.) *Developing Sustainable Leadership*. London: Paul Chapman Publishing.

Holmes, E. (2005) *Teacher Well-being*. London: RoutledgeFalmer.

Neenan, M. (2009) *Developing Resilience: A cognitive behavioural approach*. Hove: Routledge.

Part Two

Creative classroom practice

2

Chapter 3

Making the most of the mixed-experience Year 7 classroom

Caroline Conlon

Lost in transfer

> 'French is like Maths and English – you learn the basics and then you learn more about it and in more depth and detail as you get older.'
>
> (Year 7 pupil)

If only it were that easy! The 'new and exciting era for a subject that has been hovering on the margins of acceptability for many years' (Driscoll, 2014: 259) has well and truly begun. But with this new statutory subject at key stage 2 (KS2) have come further challenges for secondary school practitioners, as they strive to build effectively on the diverse range of experiences Year 7 learners bring with them in the move from KS2, where foreign language (FL) teaching and learning continue to add to an already 'complex web of established practices and beliefs' (ibid.: 259). Primary schools are responding to the statutory requirements to lay the foundations of FL learning with energy and vigour. Indeed, *Languages Trends 2014/15* (Board and Tinsley, 2015: 65) talks about the 'immediate impact both on the number of primary schools teaching a language and on the provision of many of those which already did so', noting that nearly half of all primary schools are introducing languages in key stage 1 (KS1) even though this is not a statutory requirement. The primary school FL landscape continues to shift and the picture will undoubtedly grow in complexity over the coming years.

Learners are arriving at secondary school not just with FL experience but, in many cases, with expertise that needs not only to be acknowledged but also built upon to ensure both continued motivation and progress. Though many secondary school FL teachers may have been involved in transfer and transition in their pastoral roles, it feels timely for more of them to join in conversations about subject-specific pedagogy to ensure that student motivation, engagement and progress are enhanced from the outset and throughout key stage 3 (KS3). To avoid the widely acknowledged Year 7 '"hiatus" in progress' (Galton *et al.*, 1999: 6), secondary school FL practitioners will want to harness previous experiences to engage all, as the second phase of the FL learning journey begins.

A logical response to this moment might be to enter into the school transfer dialogue with a focus on creating a 'seamless web' (Galton *et al.*, 2003): how might Year 7 teachers work to ensure that the seven-year statutory FL learning programme runs smoothly? *New Paradigm for Languages* (Dearing and King, 2007: 8) set out a very clear picture of this FL experience which might then diversify into a range of pathways at 14+. After a post-2010 election interruption, this languages learning journey has now, finally, begun. The journey's end, however, currently maintains its optional status at key stage 4 (KS4) and has slipped back into a one-size-fits-all GCSE examination, with the discussions around alternative accreditation seemingly shelved by the current government. The need to inspire all students to achieve their potential and to foster a love of languages has never been more urgent as the two new headline measures – Attainment 8 and Progress 8, along with the English Baccalaureate (EBacc) – loom ready to 'encourage' greater uptake. KS4 teachers, meanwhile, will want to inherit successful and positive language learners.

Looking back to when the *Paradigm* was shared, it is interesting to note that it ran concurrently with the launch of the Languages Ladder qualification, during a period when National Curriculum (NC) levels were tightening their grip as schools looked to their use as a means to track and report progress. For many, this assessment backdrop has served to reinforce the notion of the 'seamless web', indeed this was perhaps the original vision promoted by policymakers who pronounced that every learner should leave KS2 at an NC level 4, from where secondary schools could pick up and continue. Many secondary school teachers were asking themselves how this would work. Primary schools were encouraged and supported to devise FL programmes they could resource and that would meet their immediate needs, while secondary schools had worked hard to diversify the offer of languages at the start of KS3. What exactly would happen when Year 6 learners transferred over and had to start a new language?

Though it does not suggest a solution, the 2013 NC (Department for Education, 2013) makes explicit reference to this dynamic: KS2 teachers are required to ensure 'substantial progress in one language', on which KS3 should build 'whether pupils continue with the same language or take up a new one'. With 90 per cent of primary schools offering French (Board and Tinsley, 2015), it is probable that a significant number of Year 7 students will indeed be starting a new language. It is perhaps unsurprising, then, that a 'fresh start' looks attractive but, as Galton *et al.* (2003: 112) state, when it comes to KS2–KS3 transfer in general, it is, in fact, neither the 'seamless web' nor the 'fresh start' that provides the answer. Instead it is about 'balancing continuities and discontinuities', which requires conversations about pedagogy. Year 7 teachers need to know what has gone before so they can make informed decisions about which approaches will take the learning forward successfully for all. What is needed, therefore, is a cross-phase dialogue to ensure 'planned advances in pedagogy and acknowledgement of pupils' social maturity as well as their developing understanding of the processes of learning and of themselves as learners' (ibid.: 114).

This call has been echoed in FL quarters, where there is wide acknowledgement of the need for the growing community of FL pedagogues to establish some shared understandings of approaches to the seven-year statutory programme of study and to foster mutual respect for each other's contribution to that learning journey. Teachers from each key stage need to collaborate to ensure that learners' prior experience is identified, valued and informs KS3 planning. As empowering as it might feel to be released from the shackles of curriculum continuity – the 'seamless web' – there is still work to be done to establish who is doing what, when, how and why if we are to make the most of prior experiences and build a seven-year experience that makes sense to everyone (teachers in both phases, learners and parents or carers). This requires us not only to increase our knowledge of what is happening in each key stage but also to deepen our understanding of FL teaching and learning within the two pedagogic contexts.

As the conversations about transfer and progression in FL learning are set to begin in earnest again, let us fold up the ladders and reconvene at the bottom of what my UCL Institute of Education (IOE) colleague, Karen Turner, referred to as the 'spiral staircase'. It is an apt metaphor as teachers in KS3 cast a glance backward, to see how prior experiences might move the learners on. Spiralling, as Moore (2012: 21) says, 'rather rejects the notion of steady, incremental, step-by-step "accumulation" of knowledge: it allows and encourages the learners to take a step backwards as well as forwards, and to revise understandings by revisiting them.' It is my hope that this initial discussion will foster confidence among Year 7 teachers to realize that, whether continuing with the same language or not, all learners arrive as language learners with transferable expertise that can, and should, be acknowledged, valued and built-on to help them progress. This is a moment to capitalize explicitly on the rich language environments one often encounters in urban settings, as well as on prior curriculum-based language learning experiences, to secure both progress and motivation.

Looking back to look forward

> 'At primary school, we did games and songs, we had lots of colour pictures and now we do serious stuff, like writing and memorizing.'

> 'We do more solo learning, more writing and reading and you have to think about a lot more things – grammar, accents, pronunciation.'

> 'Yeah, now we have homework and we do tests and Miss is an experienced teacher.'

> (Y7 focus group, 2015)

Before making adjustments, the most important thing for KS3 teachers is to try to establish a clear and accurate picture of what the early foundations of the FL learning journey look like; it can't just be about 'fun' in KS2 and 'serious stuff' in KS3. While there is an urgent need for cross-phase dialogue and collaborative planning, the logistics often militate against this (arguably more so in urban settings where secondary schools inherit learners from large numbers of feeder schools). Some secondary schools, however, have identified core feeder schools with which they can build stronger links. Another way to establish cross-phase, face-to-face contact is via the Association for Language Learning (ALL) Primary Hubs (see www. all-languages.org.uk/community/local). These operate across the country and are run by primary lead teachers who bring together professionals at local level to share information, ideas and resources; the ALL website has contact details. Should such collaboration not immediately prove possible, how else might a secondary school practitioner gain a deeper understanding of policy and practice in KS2 in the meantime?

To establish a general picture of KS2 FL teaching and learning, one useful place to start is with the non-statutory *KS2 Framework* (DCSF, 2005). Launched in 2005 to support the implementation of FL entitlement, it was conceived as a means to link to existing approaches in primary school literacy lessons, and its influence on primary FL practice is obvious. This skills-focused document, with its three strands of Oracy (O), Literacy (L) and Intercultural Understanding (IU), and its cross-cutting strands of Knowledge about Language (KAL) and Language Learning Strategies (LLS), was devised as a tool to support the planning and delivery of FL-specific content within the wider context of the National Literacy Strategy. Referencing Alexander's 2012 *Cambridge Primary Review*, Driscoll (2014: 263) notes how primary teachers use the terms 'whole child' and 'whole curriculum' as a means to sum up the primary pedagogical ethos. FLs have been introduced in primary schools with an emphasis on broader language and literacy skills, and on learner confidence with language in general. FLs in this context are not subject to the close, subject-specific tracking that is commonplace in many secondary schools, where content delivery in preparation for final assessment can dominate. It is more about teaching children to do a lot with a little and to make links with all the languages in their lives, with KAL often taking precedence. As Helen Groothues, former CILT Primary Language Teacher Adviser, commented in a recent personal email exchange:

> For me, the essence of Primary FL teaching and learning is that in primary school the foreign language can become part of the fabric of school life, rather than a discreet subject to be taught in doses. The FL can be woven into all areas of the curriculum.

If we think of substantial progress more in terms of each learner's wider literacy profile, we can start to build bridges between KS2 and KS3 and manage what Jane Jones (Chapter 1) refers to as the continuity–discontinuity dichotomy. Arguably, a shift away from the content to the skills agenda, as originally envisaged in the now largely discarded KS3 Framework (DCSF, 2010), still offers a possible way forward and could support teams in helping colleagues, learners and parents to understand that starting a new language at KS3 should not necessarily put learners at a disadvantage. If the profile of transferable skills is raised, then the exciting range of languages offered at the outset of KS3 should be retained as teams seek to build on prior learning. Just as Hunt *et al.* (quoted in Jones and Coffey, 2013: 157) said over ten years ago, 'an emphasis on transferable language learning skills may help where children begin a new language at secondary school.'

Comparing the 2005 non-statutory KS2 Framework, in particular KAL and LLS (see Tables 3.1 and 3.2 in the appendix to this chapter), with the current statutory KS2 Programme of Study (see Table 3.3 in the appendix to this chapter for Rachel Hawkes' very helpful overview), clear links can be seen. It seems likely that the number of learners arriving with an understanding of key language concepts such as the gender of nouns or adjectival agreements will continue to grow. As KS2 FLs become more secure, learners are likely not only to be able to identify key parts of speech such as verbs, but might well know that they have to be conjugated, and be familiar the role of pronouns. It is exciting to think that the Year 7 classroom will increasingly be inhabited by learners who have been taught to listen attentively and can cope with segments of unpredictable language, while also knowing how to break words down to be able to pronounce them accurately.

Year 7 teachers can use this to build on the familiar, as they also begin to introduce new challenges such as classrooms dominated by the target language (TL), to establish what Christie (2016: 74) describes as the 'target language lifestyle'. He refers to classrooms where routines are conducted in the TL and where learners are supported to not only engage in pre-rehearsed conversations but also speak with increasing spontaneity. Moving from the familiar to the new, learners will discover that verbs not only change depending on who is completing the action but also on when it was completed, as they are taught to identify and use tenses. Again, the overview of the KS2 and KS3 NC shows (Table 3.3) how progression between the two key stages can be secured if there is a shift from language-specific content to transferable language learning skills. Conversations about process need to take precedence over product.

Careful planning, cross-curricular links with colleagues from English and English as an additional language (EAL) and an eye to wider school literacy initiatives will allow KS3 FL teachers to establish the right blend of English and TL use as they seek to balance continuity and discontinuity across the two key stages. Reminiscent of Hawkins' Languages Awareness programme (1987), this collaborative model has the potential to support pupils in developing a greater sense of themselves as successful language learners, recognizing their range of skills from broad experiences as valuable assets.

Lastly, the government-funded ALL Connect project is another important source of information (www.all-languages.org.uk/teaching/initiatives/all-connect-3). Launched in 2014 across three regions, the project has so far generated resources for the successful implementation of the revised KS2 and KS3 programmes of study, with transition featuring as a key theme. Resources are freely available online via the ALL Connect blog; of particular interest are the KS2 Transition Toolkit and KS2–3 Transition modules (see https://allconnectblog.wordpress.com/category/ks2-3-transition) with their associated training materials.

Planned advances in pedagogy: Learning from the learners

As Year 7 begins, many schools use questionnaires to establish the basic facts about learners' prior experiences. Tests are also used to establish some baseline data for school tracking purposes but will, of course, disadvantage those starting a new language. I would suggest, however, that neither of these is a substitute for some early diagnostic approaches in the Y7 classroom. The start to KS3 provides an opportune moment for a diagnosis of prior learning to inform future planning, something that will have an impact not only on what is taught but also on how it is approached.

The topic 'Myself', for example, is the most natural place to start in the first few lessons of Year 7 and is often introduced via the drilling of a TL question-and-answer about names, alongside an introduction to the TL alphabet (a model generally proposed by KS3 textbooks). This is, however, problematic in the mixed experience classroom where many will be very confident with this familiar approach and language, while others are meeting new content, though not necessarily a new set of concepts. One solution might be a move away from the traditional present-practice-produce (the 3Ps) approach, to *doing* – what Johnson (2008: 275) calls 'the deep-end strategy'. Learners are set a communication challenge and encouraged to communicate with available resources in pairs or small groups. The Year 7 teacher can monitor responses, teasing out which elements need to be presented and practised after that. As an inclusive approach that allows for a differentiated response to meet the needs of both those who are new to the language and those who are not, it also serves to inspire a natural discussion about strategies and transferable skills. This shift of focus from content to skills and strategy, from product to process, will allow FL teachers to continue the discussion about the 'how', alongside the 'what'. This is a potentially powerful way to encourage greater learner independence, thus enhancing their capacity for autonomy.

As KS3 teachers make plans to revisit language concepts such as articles and gender, a similar task-based approach could be adopted. Rather than teaching the class a list of domestic animals with a view to talking about pets, learners might draw up of lists of animals they already know before putting these into categories. This could provide a springboard into the teaching of a new vocabulary, perhaps set within a new context such as wild animals and their habitats, or animal groups to link with science. Such an approach bridges the gap between the familiar and unfamiliar, to include and to stretch as appropriate. Perhaps this could also be combined with the injection of language to express more complex ideas – language with high-transfer value, as highlighted in the KS3 Framework for languages. For example: 'I have seen a ... but never a ...' or 'I would like to see ...' rather than the standard 'I have' or more commonly in our city schools, 'I don't have' (*'Je n'ai pas de …'*), followed by the name of a pet and thereby introducing quite a complex language point in French almost by accident!

Similarly, by moving away from the notion of word-sentence-paragraph to define progression, early KS3 teachers should feel confident that more experienced FL learners have the capacity to cope with longer passages, both to enjoy and to analyse. During KS2, they may well have listened to, and read, longer items as their teachers sought to develop a wide set of language learning skills, without over-emphasizing comprehension. Potentially, the learners will have enjoyed stories, songs, poems and rhymes as they were encouraged to explore the patterns and sounds of the FL and introduced to culture, thus expanding their LLS, KAL and IU.

These examples of pedagogical shifts could also potentially have a significant impact on motivation. Dörnyei and Csizér (1998) outline ten commandments for motivating learners and these shifts could address several of these. By setting up classroom scenarios that allow learners to show what they think they can do using their prior experiences and expertise, Year 7 teachers can increase learners' linguistic self-confidence. By building on interest rather than tests or grades and by developing curiosity by introducing the unexpected – that is, by carefully balancing the familiar and unfamiliar – the teacher can make the language classes interesting. As learners work together to take responsibility for their own learning, and by being in control, using their creativity and imagination, their capacity for autonomy can be enhanced. The diagnostic approaches and subsequent needs analysis will allow teachers to get to know their classes quickly and thus prepare lessons that are personally relevant, based on personalization of the learning process from the outset. By building on KS2 approaches to longer written and spoken items, and in response to the demands of the 2013 KS3 NC, learners' familiarization with the TL culture can continue to be developed.

In summary, what I am calling for is a more mixed diet, an early offer that breaks free from the more traditional conceptualization of progression which so often provides a ceiling for learners who are trapped at word level, unable to show off their skills, whether starting a new language or not. Urban classrooms are often full of experienced, confident language users whose transferable skills are available for their FL teachers to capitalize on as the process rather than the final product is moved into the spotlight. Let's introduce Year 7s to more language where skills outside of comprehension are highlighted and valued, and where confidence to work with the unpredictable is nurtured. A shift away from the transactional syllabus, giving students the opportunity to explore language in new contexts such as literature, stories and film, will allow secondary school teachers to use familiar approaches while launching the less familiar, such as the TL lifestyle. These are small shifts with the potential to make a significant difference.

Case study

Over the last year, the UCL IOE postgraduate certificate in education (PGCE) team has worked closely with The Regent High School (RHS), an 11–19 co-educational, mixed local authority (LA)-maintained comprehensive in the London Borough of Camden. The parents, headteacher and head of languages gave me permission to report on the approach to transfer taken by the school, to visit some Year 7 FL lessons and to speak to a small focus group of Year 7 students. The following case study provides some interesting and thought-provoking ideas for potential shifts in approaches.

In September 2014, RHS received 140 Year 7 students from 25 primary feeder schools, five of which provided the majority of the cohort and were identified by the school as their core feeders. On its website, the school highlights its 'Strong relationship with feeder primary schools including master classes, taster sessions and educational workshops', as well as its 'Friendship afternoon to welcome prospective Year 7 students and their parents' as examples of what makes it unique. Like many others, this is a secondary school striving to strike a balance between the administrative, pastoral and academic challenges of the KS2–KS3 transfer moment.

Cross-phase links

When resources allowed, the school released the head of languages to work alongside the LA's KS2 modern foreign languages (MFL) adviser and later to support the national KS3 Framework programme. During this phase, the LA developed an online French and Spanish KS2 scheme of work, and primary non-specialists were supported with training and visits to their classrooms to model delivery. Listening and speaking were areas where most support was requested. Primary and secondary school teachers visited one another's classrooms to deepen an understanding of each other's practices. A Year 6 post SATs summer term International Artists project was launched across all primary schools involving the study (in English) of a French-, German- or Spanish-speaking artist, to develop IU and linked to KS2 Art learning objectives. The aim was that local secondary FL teams could then use this as a springboard into FL work during the autumn of Year 7 – an example of the fusion of continuity and discontinuity – as the school took something familiar to explore in a new context and used it as a way into FL language objectives. RHS further reinforced KS2–KS3 links though its music project, during which Year 7 students accompanied a music teacher to two core feeder schools to work on FL songs every week, a project which culminated in a shared summer term singing event. Overall, this was an innovative cross-phase, cross-curricular project that strengthened links at a variety of levels.

To allow for transfer of information about progress, a common online assessment scheme was created by the LA for Year 6 teachers to share details of pupil progress in both writing and speaking on the virtual learning environment (VLE) online platform. While the ambitious plan to include clips of learners demonstrating their speaking skills did not come to fruition before the initiative stalled with the change of government in 2010, it remains ready for launch should resourcing allow in the future.

Before joining the school, prospective Year 7 pupils are asked to identify, in consultation with their Year 6 teachers, whether they would like to study French or Spanish. This is a flexible and responsive approach which engenders an immediate sense of investment and ownership – crucial ingredients in terms of motivation and engagement. The small focus group of Year 7 students we met comprised four who had made a deliberate choice to continue with their French and four who had no prior experience. Their comments reflect the variety of motives behind the choices they make about which language to pursue in KS3:

'I chose French because I am from Morocco. I already know English and Arabic ... It can help me when I get to Morocco plus when I go France as well.'

'To get into university you need to know a language and I want to build on what I knew already ... If I change, then it will just take me longer to get fluent.'

'Because I did it in primary school, I was a lot more comfortable with it.'

'I already speak Spanish, so now I am starting French and then I will do Italian and Portuguese.'

'I am starting French because my friends did it and two of my cousins do it.'

(Year 7 focus group participants)

Learning about the learners

Although close links with colleagues and an active transition room on the LA VLE have the potential to enhance information-gathering about individual learners, the head of department (HoD) feels the diagnostic approaches used in the induction phase and early stages of the autumn term at secondary school play a crucial, and potentially more significant, role in not only getting to know new classes but also in planning to meet their diverse range of needs. The first two weeks are used as a school-wide settling/diagnostic phase where all pupils are observed by teaching assistants who follow the class throughout the day, aiming to supplement information provided by primary schools. During this phase, any student who feels they have made the wrong language choice, or is identified by the class teachers as having potentially done so, is offered a chance to change. Since the learners only study one language as part of the curriculum at RHS, the team considers it essential for students and their families to feel they have made the right choice from the outset. This approach has been adopted recently to replace a carousel model, which was not felt to serve the subject well within the wider school assessment processes.

Plainly, the team has reflected and made some radical decisions as a means to support both the learners and the subject, and many families make the most of the chance to make an informed choice during the summer term of Year 6. These innovative developments are used in preference to starting the new phase with a test, something the team is keen to avoid as they seek to settle learners into their new setting and work to enhance confidence and risk-taking in their lessons. RHS acknowledges that this flexible model, something rarely seen, is made possible with an FL team who can all offer both French and Spanish and because of the vertical tutor groups, which allow for movement among subject teaching groups.

Again, it is interesting to talk to the learners themselves, and when I asked one boy how he came to be in his French group, he responded: 'More experienced in it. I changed from Spanish at RHS back to French because I missed it and Spanish was too hard.' This was someone who was enjoying revisiting some familiar language in new contexts, being the 'expert' in the room and relishing the challenge of being expected to extend his knowledge and skills from the outset.

Adjustments

The autumn term schemes of work have been rewritten to include the first two parts of a Language Awareness module, written and delivered after discussions with EAL and English colleagues. This is another successful cross-curricular collaboration which raises the profile of the department in contributing to the whole-school focus on language, literacy and communication. This module sits within two units: Our World and International Artists, both aimed at launching the specific FL learning objectives. Over ten weeks and 20 lessons, the team plans lessons to find out about students' home languages and their KS2 language experiences, to explore what makes a good language learner and to extend KAL and LLS. The units are structured to extend pupils' cultural knowledge about the countries where the TL is spoken. Though comparisons between the languages of the group and those they have had experience of in KS2 may be made in English, the team establishes a TL lifestyle from the outset and there is a careful, planned balance between the use of English and the TL in, and across, the lessons:

> 'The teacher speaks to us in French which is harder, well it was hard at first but now we can do it, we are getting there now.'

> 'When Miss talks in French, we have to guess what she is saying but now it is getting easier … I use my knowledge of English and Spanish to help.'

> (Year 7 pupils)

What stands out is the wealth of opportunities teachers have to plan lessons to meet the needs of all during this initial phase. There is evidence of both word-level work with the reinforcement of sound–spelling links and text-level work to extend language learner strategies in reading and listening – here the team dips back into KS2 approaches and content but moves the learning on. A range of spoken and written tasks is differentiated according to experience, interest and ability. Cross-curricular opportunities and cross-school links are reinforced via the Artists unit, which emerged as a favourite when I asked about revisiting a familiar theme from primary school:

> 'Artists was good to help us with basics and to learn how to learn properly.'

> 'Yeah, because we can use what we know and then expand, you can add what you already know so you get "outstanding effort", then Miss shares our ideas with everyone when we make a suggestion about what else we could add.'

> (Year 7 pupils)

A particular highlight for the class teacher last autumn was the moment a student produced his version of Monet's *Water Lilies*, now on display in his new setting – much to his and his teacher's delight! The students seem happy to revisit and show off their knowledge when the context has shifted and their expertise is both acknowledged and extended, as another Year 7 pupil commented: 'You can refresh it. It stays in your brain and you will never forget it.' This does, however, require a skilful management of the transfer continuity–discontinuity dichotomy, as the class teacher makes careful, informed decisions about how to strike a balance between the familiar and unfamiliar.

The French lessons I visited took place during the summer term when the class was midway through the five-week-long 'Storytelling' unit, which also includes the third and final part of the Year 7 Language Awareness programme. At this point the learning spiral not only dips back into KS2 but back to the start of the Y7 scheme of work too. The class was made up of 26 students: 16 girls and 10 boys from 14 primary schools, and one mid-year arrival from Spain. Five are recorded as having English as their home language, the others have eight other languages shared between them: Amharic, Arabic, Bengali, Farsi, French, Lingala, Spanish and Somali.

KS2 FL experiences varied considerably, with 14 pupils having received some French teaching, five some Spanish and one some Italian, while others stated they had not done any FL work in primary school. According to the learners, their FL entitlement had been delivered in a wide range of ways, from once a week for an hour from Reception to Year 6, to a short taster in Year 3 until the French speaking teaching assistant left. This diversity of experience will be familiar to many secondary teachers in schools where enquiries about previous experience are made; there can be no assumptions about what the offer has looked like, even when learners have studied the same language.

Students were working on Little Red Riding Hood – *Le Chaperon Rouge*. The ten lessons are structured to expose learners to authentic materials to give them a chance to put their LLS and KAL into practice, as they work across a range of tasks with both shorter and extended spoken and written texts, including a challenging authentic text. At the start of every half term the class is organized into mixed ability, mixed experience groups with rotating roles being shared out more and more strategically as the teacher gets to know her class. Each group has a team leader, a team leader (*chef d'équipe*), a spokesperson (*rapporteur*), at least one linguist/language adviser (*linguiste*) and a monitor to oversee proceedings (*moniteur*). This is an example of one way in which the teacher opts to continue with an approach with which learners will be familiar from primary school but not often seen in secondary MFL classrooms; it is popular too:

> 'I like talking to the others and working in pairs and groups – I find it hard to work on my own ... when we do it together we do it better.'
>
> (Y7 girl)

Collaboration, cooperation and strategies to memorize new language were highlighted as the key lesson objectives, with praise and rewards being offered for group rather than individual successes on this occasion. The starter activity required learners to make three sentences which, once checked for understanding, were to be committed to memory. Groups had three nouns and three verbs to work with – '*les yeux, les oreilles, les dents*', '*entendre, manger, voir*' – linked by '*pour*'. Someone calling out, 'Miss I can see a pattern,' gave the teacher the perfect link she needed to move the discussion on to 'how' the new language was being committed to memory. This is where the class was able to demonstrate their considerable expertise as experienced language learners and users, with every group's 'rapporteur' (spokesperson) offering a wide range of ideas, including: saying it out loud to myself/my partner a lot, using the primary school 'copy/cover/copy' approach to write it down, testing each other, saying over and over again in my head etc. During the group work, I overheard one student share his thoughts with his group:

> 'English helps with reading and writing but not with the talking and listening – *fleurs* and flowers was easy to guess when you read it but not when you hear it.'
>
> (Y7 boy)

The whole class discussion also provided the students with a chance to say when and how they use these strategies elsewhere in their learning – again, communication skills across the curriculum. Moving on to more complex phrases in preparation for the final outcome of the unit, the re-enactment of a scene from the play using French from memory, the class did some reading work where sound–spelling links were highlighted and reinforced. The teacher then introduced the class to a key strategy to support memorizing, that of 'initializing', a technique often used in primary schools and with which the class was familiar and comfortable, as made explicit by one boy: 'Miss, we done this in Year 6 in English.'

Slide 1

Le loup ou le PCR?

C'est pour mieux te voir, mon enfant!

Oh grand-mère, que vous avez de grands yeux!

Entre, mon enfant.

Oh grand-mère, que vous avez de grandes dents!

C'est Petit Chaperon rouge, grand-mère.

C'est pour mieux te manger, mon enfant!

Qui est là?

Qui parle? Who says what?

Le loup
PCR

C'est pour mieux t'entendre, mon enfant!

Oh grand-mère, que vous avez de grandes oreilles!

Slide 2

Dialogue

Oh grand-mère, que vous avez de grands yeux!

Qui est là?

C'est pour mieux te voir, mon enfant!

Oh grand-mère, que vous avez de grandes dents!

C'est Petit Chaperon rouge, grand-mère.

Oh grand-mère, que vous avez de grandes oreilles!

C'est pour mieux te manger, mon enfant!

Entre, mon enfant.

C'est pour mieux t'entendre, mon enfant!

Slide 3

Memorising strategy:
Initialising

1. Qel?
2. CPCr, gm.
3. E,me.
4. Og-m, qvadgy!
5. Cepmtv, me!
6. Ogm, qvadgo!
7. Cepmte, me!
8. Ogm, qvadgd!
9. Cepmtm, me!

Slide 4

Dialogue

Le loup	Le Petit Chaperon Rouge
• 1.Qel?	• 1.CPCr, gm.
• 2. E,me.	• 2.Og-m, qvadgy!
• 3. Cepmtv, me!	• 3. Ogm, qvadgo!
• 4. Cepmte, me!	• 4. Ogm, qvadgd!
• 5. Cepmtm, me!	

Figure 3.1: Little Red Riding Hood PowerPoint slides

Copies of the four slides (see Figure 3.1) show how the process unfolds, with the written support gradually being removed to aid memory. Once again, we can see how the teacher treads that careful line between the familiar and unfamiliar, using a familiar approach in a new context, carefully marking her moves from French TL to English as she encourages the class to explore their strategic thinking. Interestingly, this unit had originally featured in the autumn term to make a close link to KS2 storytelling techniques but has recently been moved to the end of the year to give the students an opportunity to revisit and extend their LLS, KAL and IU while working with a challenging authentic text. The progression is not lost on the students, as I was told by one pupil:

> 'Yeah, Artists was good to help us with the basics and then with the other topics we worked harder and did sentences and then speaking and now we are doing reading a story, it's everything – it has got harder as the year went on but we can do it, we are good!'
>
> (Year 7 boy)

And the unit is a popular one. As one Year 7 boy commented: 'Yeah, the *Chaperon Rouge* play was really fun. I like working in groups.'

Next steps at RHS

When asked about future hopes for their language study, the focus group thought that a fully-funded trip on the Eurostar to Paris might be nice, and they were very keen to know more about the people and country. They wanted to learn the language they might need when asking for directions, for help and for going shopping. The HoD was interested to hear that the students were asking for more transactional, real-life scenario, language such as that traditionally examined in the GCSE. She wondered if the balance in her revised scheme of work was not quite right yet in terms of building on prior learning, and whether she needed to introduce language that casted forward to the final assessment sooner (discontinuity to maintain engagement in Year 8, perhaps, echoing Galton's ideas). And starting something new to engage the students as well as acknowledging and building on prior learning would ensure that she could also provide continuity.

There was also a request for more current affairs in French, something to help to get ready for Euro 2016 and more French accents from around the world, such as Canadian French. There was the potential here to do more work on listening attentively, perhaps without the need to comprehend. This was a motivated group who were seeing their FL studies within much broader contexts and were confident as they shared their 'meanings that matter' (Dearing and King, 2007: 15). Another area for the MFL team to think about is the potential to make more explicit reference to the actual language learnt in KS2; it came as a surprise to one learner who had swapped from KS2 Spanish to KS3 French to learn that gendered nouns were common to both languages.

Casting forward

As secondary schools get to grips with the revised GCSE syllabuses, this seems like an ideal moment to begin to look back to plan ahead, rather than allowing the assessment backwash to dictate. As this case study shows, collaboration both between, and within, schools can foster a reflective and responsive approach for the benefit of all. These changes have been made over a period of time and it is important that KS3 teams do not feel paralysed by the heavy weight of change currently being managed. Dörnyei and Csizér (1998: 208) call for a 'motivationally conscious teaching approach' as a way to support all pupils to become successful language learners, something many of the initiatives outlined here share. I firmly believe that these shifts at the outset of Year 7 have the potential to pay big dividends. This early investment at the start of the secondary school FL learning journey could well provide the carrot to counterbalance what runs the risk of becoming the stick of EBacc, Progress 8 and Attainment 8.

Acknowledgement

With grateful thanks to Najoua Hilali, Head of Languages, RHS, and her Year 7 French class.

Questions for practice

- To what extent are you, or other FL team members, involved in transfer initiatives within your school? What is the potential for you to be involved in discussions about both pastoral and academic subject-specific links?
- What more can you do to develop your awareness of, or involvement in, local networks of FL pedagogues, or national networks via the Association of Language Learning?
- What adjustments might you make to your Year 7 (autumn term at least) offer in the light of your students' *prior* learning?

Further reading

1. Language learning strategies

Practice:
Harris, V. (2002) 'Learning to learn: Strategy instruction in the modern languages classroom'. In Swarbrick, A. (ed.) *Aspects of Teaching Secondary Modern Foreign Languages: Perspectives on practice*. London: RoutledgeFalmer, 3–22.

Theory:
Cohen, A.D. and Macaro, E. (eds) (2007) *Language Learner Strategies: Thirty years of research and practice*. Oxford: Oxford University Press.

2. Assessment for learning

Jones, J. (2010) 'The role of Assessment for Learning in the management of primary to secondary transition: Implications for language teachers'. *Language Learning Journal,* 38 (2), 175–91.

3. Speaking

Christie, C. (2016) 'Speaking spontaneously in the modern foreign languages classroom: Tools for supporting successful target language conversation'. *Language Learning Journal,* 44 (1), 74–89.

References

Association for Language Learning – ALL Connect. Online. www.all-languages.org.uk/teaching/initiatives/all-connect-3 (accessed 17 June 2016).

Association for Language Learning – All Connect blog. Online. https://allconnectblog.wordpress.com (accessed 17 June 2016).

Association for Language Learning Primary Hubs. Online. www.all-languages.org. uk/community/local (accessed 17 June 2016).

Board, K. and Tinsley, T. (2015) *Language Trends 2014/15: The state of language learning in primary and secondary schools in England.* Reading: CfBT Education Trust. Online. www.britishcouncil.org/sites/default/files/language_trends_survey_2015.pdf (accessed 27 May 2015).

Christie, C. (2016) 'Speaking spontaneously in the modern foreign languages classroom: Tools for supporting successful target language conversation'. *Language Learning Journal,* 44 (1), 4–89.

DCSF (2005) *The KS2 Framework for Languages.* Online. http://webarchive.nationalarchives.gov.uk/20130401151715/http://www.education.gov.uk/publications/standard/publicationDetail/Page1/DFES%20 1721%202005 (accessed 17 June 2016).

— (2010) *The KS3 Framework for Languages.* Online. http://webarchive. nationalarchives.gov.uk/20110511211850/http://nationalstrategies.standards. dcsf.gov.uk/search/secondary/results/nav:46155 (accessed 15 August 2015).

Dearing, R. and King, L. (2007) *Languages Review.* Annesley: DfES. Online. http:// webarchive.nationalarchives.gov.uk/20130401151715/http://www.teachernet. gov.uk/_doc/11124/LanguageReview.pdf (accessed 27 May 2015).

Department for Education (2013) *Statutory Guidance – National Curriculum in England: Languages programmes of study.* Online. http://tinyurl.com/jryuc82 (accessed 27 May 2016).

Dörnyei, Z. and Csizér, K. (1998) 'Ten commandments for motivating language learners: Results of an empirical study'. *Language Teaching Research*, 2 (3), 203–29.

Driscoll, P. (2014) 'A new era for primary languages'. In Driscoll, P., Macaro, E. and Swarbrick, A. (eds), *Debates in Modern Languages Education.* Abingdon: Routledge.

Galton, M., Gray, J. and Ruddock, J. (1999) *The Impact of School Transfer on Pupil Progress and Attainment.* London: DfES. Research report 131. Online. www.musicalbridges.org.uk/wp-content/uploads/2014/07/The-Impact-of-School-Transitions-and-Transfers-Galton-et-al-1999-.pdf (accessed 22 July 2015).

— (2003) *Transfer and Transitions in the Middle Years of Schooling (7–14): Continuities and discontinuities in learning.* London: DfES. Online. www.lotc.org.uk/wp-content/uploads/2010/12/DfES-Research-Report-RR443-2003.pdf (accessed 27 May 2016).

Hawkes, R. (2014) *Transition Presentations.* Online. www.rachelhawkes.com/PandT/2014_Curriculum/2014Curr.php (accessed 13 July 2016).

Hawkins, E. (1987) *Modern Languages in the Curriculum.* Cambridge: CUP.

Johnson, K. (2008) *An Introduction to Foreign Language Learning and Teaching,* 2nd edn. Abingdon: Routledge.

Jones, J. and Coffey, S. (2013) *Modern Foreign Languages 5–11: A guide for teachers,* 2nd edn. London: Routledge.

Moore, A. (2012) *Teaching and Learning: Pedagogy, curriculum and culture.* London: Routledge.

Appendix

Table 3.1: KS2 Framework – Knowledge about Language: Overview of Years 3–6

• When learning a new language, children reinforce and reinterpret knowledge and understanding gained in learning their first language(s). • In the early years children should develop insights into the sounds and some of the structures of the new language and compare them with their own language(s). • As they increase their understanding of the rules of sounds, spellings and grammar, they should begin to apply these rules when creating new language, both spoken and written. • As they progress, children should have frequent opportunities to apply previously learnt knowledge and rules in English and the new language. • Children will have experience of learning about and using simple grammatical terms such as nouns, verbs, adjectives, adverbs and pronouns. They will need to apply this knowledge in the context of learning about languages which are new to them. • This knowledge can be taught in the new language or in English.	Children should have opportunities to: • Identify phonemes, letters and words which are similar to and different from English in spoken and written forms • Recognise commonly used rhyming sounds and learn how they are written • Understand and use a range of common words from all word classes, especially verbs • Recognize that languages use different writing systems, have different ways of expressing social relationships (politeness), borrow words from other languages and describe concepts and ideas differently • Apply their knowledge of language rules and conventions when building short sentences and texts, spoken and written • Understand and use question forms and negatives in spoken and written language • Understand that rules and conventions are respected by native speakers and are important for learners • Recognise some basic aspects of agreement where relevant, e.g. gender, singular/plural, pronoun/verb, adjectives • Recognise the importance and significance of intonation and punctuation.

(DCSF, 2005: 78)

Table 3.2: Language Learning Strategies: Overview of Years 3–6

• An important aim of language learning in Key Stage 2 is to familiarise children with strategies which they can apply to the learning of any language.	Children should have opportunities to: • Discuss their language learning and try out different learning strategies • Plan and prepare for language learning activities, analysing what they need in order to carry out a task
• In the early stages children should develop an awareness of some of the basic approaches to learning a new language which they will be using, e.g. imitating, memorising, repeating and practising, using mime and gesture, asking for repetition. • As they increase their competence in the new language, they will be able to apply learning strategies to help them use known language in new contexts, identify key words and phrases in speech and in simple written texts and use word lists and dictionaries. • Children can be helped to see how they have used language learning strategies in the acquisition of their first language(s), how they are using them in learning the new language and how they might use them in future language learning as well as in more general learning in other areas of the curriculum.	• Use gesture and mime to show they understand and to help make themselves understood • Identify techniques to develop pronunciation, e.g. observing native speakers, speaking aloud, making recordings • Improve their ability to memorise, using a range of strategies such as association with a physical response, word association, rhyme and rhythm and visualisation • Identify techniques which assist understanding, e.g. looking at the face of the speaker, asking for repetition or clarification, listening for key words • Sort and categorise known words and investigate the characteristics of new language • Apply prior knowledge of language structure(s) when attempting to understand unknown language or to create new language • Use monolingual and bilingual dictionaries.

(DCSF, 2005: 84)

Table 3.3: 2013 National Curriculum overview grid

KS2	KS3
Listening • **Listen attentively** to spoken language and show understanding by joining in and responding. • Explore the patterns and sounds of language through songs and rhymes and **link the spelling, sound and meaning of words.**	Listening • Listen to **a variety of forms of spoken language** to obtain information and respond appropriately. • **Transcribe** words and short sentences that they hear with increasing accuracy.
Speaking • **Engage in conversations;** ask and answer questions; express opinions and respond to those of others; seek clarification and help. • **Speak in sentences,** using familiar vocabulary, phrases and basic language structures. • **Develop accurate pronunciation and intonation** so that others understand when they are reading aloud or using familiar words and phrases. • Present ideas and information orally to a range of audiences.	Speaking • **Initiate and develop conversations,** coping with unfamiliar language and unexpected responses, making use of important social conventions such as formal modes of address. • **Express and develop ideas clearly** and with increasing accuracy, both orally and in writing. • **Speak coherently and confidently, with increasingly accurate pronunciation and intonation.**
Reading • **Read** carefully and show understanding of **words, phrases and simple writing.** • **Appreciate stories, songs, poems and rhymes in the language.** • Broaden their vocabulary and develop their ability to understand new words that are introduced into familiar written material, including through using a dictionary.	Reading • **Read** and show comprehension of **original and adapted materials from a range of different sources,** understanding the purpose, important ideas and details, and **provide an accurate English translation of short, suitable material.**

- Read literary texts in the
language, such as stories,
songs, poems and letters,
to stimulate ideas, develop
creative expression and
expand understanding of the
language and culture.

Writing
- **Write phrases from memory,
and adapt these** to create
new sentences, to express
ideas clearly.
- Describe people, places,
things and actions orally
and in writing.

Grammar
- **Understand basic grammar**
appropriate to the language
being studied, such as
(where relevant): feminine,
masculine and neuter forms
and the conjugation of
high-frequency verbs; key
features and patterns of
the language; how to apply
these, for instance, to build
sentences; and how these
differ from or are similar
to English.

Writing
- **Write prose using an
increasingly wide range of
grammar and vocabulary,
write creatively to express
their own ideas and
opinions, and translate short
written text accurately into
the foreign language.**

Grammar
- **Identify and use tenses**
or other structures which
convey the present, past, and
future as appropriate to the
language being studied.
- Use and manipulate a
**variety of key grammatical
structures** and patterns,
including voices and moods,
as appropriate.
- Develop and **use a wide-
ranging and deepening
vocabulary** that goes beyond
their immediate needs and
interests, allowing them to
give and justify opinions and
take part in discussion about
wider issues.
- Use accurate grammar,
spelling and punctuation.

(Hawkes, 2014)

Chapter 4

Using literature in the key stage 3 modern foreign languages classroom

Fotini Diamantidaki

Context

Over the last 50 years or so, foreign language teaching and learning have seen various methods and approaches come and go. In the Grammar Translation method, the written word and accuracy were important, often at the expense of real communication and context. Literature extracts featured in textbooks on the method but there was the danger that it was part of an elitist and intellectual pursuit. During the 1970s and 1980s, teaching for communication came to the fore. The study of literature was generally confined to advanced level, as at lower levels more instrumental functions of the language with so-called communicative value were prioritized.

Now, recent changes to the National Curriculum (NC) in England have promoted what might be considered more traditional elements of modern foreign languages (MFL) teaching and learning, including the study of literary texts:

- understand and respond to spoken and written language from a variety of authentic sources ...
- discover and develop an appreciation of a range of writing in the language studied ...
- read and show comprehension of original and adapted materials from a range of different sources
- read literary texts in the language [such as stories, songs, poems and letters], to stimulate ideas, develop creative expression and expand understanding of the language and culture.

(DfE, 2013: 1–2)

By the end of key stage 3 (KS3), pupils are expected 'to understand and communicate personal and factual information that goes beyond their immediate needs and interests, developing and justifying points of view in speech and writing, with increased spontaneity, independence and accuracy. The entire process should also provide suitable preparation for further study' (DFE, 2013: 2).

Literature aside, reading has been highlighted as a neglected skill area in MFL lessons (Mitchell, 2008), where young readers 'adopt a word-by-word processing approach which makes it very difficult for them to read for pleasure' (Ellis and Shintani, 2014: 172). Building confidence is therefore essential for the students to see words in context and to read longer passages. Literature is to be considered as a tool as well as an end in itself (Hişmanoğlu, 2005) in the context of MFL teaching and learning.

In the light of these factors, the chapter proposes that literature can be used to reinforce and develop reading skills and develop linguistic proficiency (Ellis and Shintani, 2014). It can also provide additional input, which will allow the learner to appreciate the complexity of the language, going beyond the learning of isolated items of vocabulary.

Why teach literature in the foreign language classroom?

One of the reasons for integrating literature is that it is real language produced by a real writer for a real audience, designed to convey a real message. This characterizes literature as authentic material (Morrow, 1979), with authenticity not being a property residing in the text itself, but conceived more like a process of authentication, triggered by a reader. 'Authentic', therefore, is used to describe the 'specific ways in which language is made communicatively appropriate to context' (Widdowson, 2003: 93). Widdowson continues by saying that it is 'people who make a text real by realising it as discourse, that is to say by relating to specific contexts of communal cultural values and attitudes' (ibid.: 98). The notion of transferability and a re-creation of cultural reality according to any evolving context, in Widdowson's words, lead us to the next reason for integrating literary texts into the foreign language classroom, namely cultural enrichment.

Literature can help the reader appreciate more deeply the lifestyle of the country of the target language (TL) they are studying. While it is also possible to do this with radio and newspapers, literature is a more 'intimate' approach because even if the characters, for example in a novel, are fictitious, a literary text can provide a context in which characters from different social backgrounds associate with the reality of the reader. The reader can explore the thoughts, feelings, habits and customs, beliefs and fears of a population of a particular context and start making links with their own reality. This is just as powerful as engaging with contexts that might deal with the more immediate concerns of learners.

Another quality of the literary text is that the reader gains a wealth of vocabulary and can enrich their lexical knowledge. As Collie and Slater argue, 'the compressed quality of much literary language produces unexpected density of meaning' (Collie and Slater, 1987: 5). Literature provides a rich context in which elements of the lexicon or syntax can be highlighted during the teaching process. A first reading can also help the reader become familiar with the different styles of language, see the variety of possible structures and understand new meanings of words and phrases, drawing on the context and personal interpretations. A more detailed reading of a text may allow students to make assumptions about the meaning of the linguistic elements and deduce the meaning of a text as a whole. The overall aim in this process is for the learner to achieve 'foreign language competence' (Thom Thom, 2008: 121) through 'a dynamic, student-centred approach' (Hişmanoğlu, 2005: 57).

Finally, literature has the capacity to motivate learners by engaging their imagination and creativity, and generating emotion (as explored by Simon Coffey in Chapter 5). These are elements that can capture the learners' interest and create an atmosphere in which they can learn how to use the vocabulary and structures they are being taught, in a less 'mechanical' way. Using literature may be a useful alternative to motivating learners to work from texts made specifically for pedagogical purposes.

Integrating literature into the curriculum

Due to a lack of curriculum time and the pressure to demonstrate clear learning outcomes, many colleagues may be reluctant to devote much time to literature-related work. One way to introduce literature is to integrate it into topics that are commonly taught, such as family, seasons, school, education or items of clothing. The integration of the literary text is therefore suggested as one of the teaching resources used during the teaching process and not as a one-off task. Choosing appropriate texts for specific topics – a pre-defined set of topics that schools have to cover for GCSE in whichever language – will allow the learners to develop more complex skills in reading within the particular topic area, see the language in context and, finally, with the right guidance, go beyond the survival stage of communication and 'ultimately increase their reading proficiency' (MacKay, 1982: 529).

The following case study illustrates the integration of topics by sharing some French, Spanish, Russian and Chinese literature. I suggest that if a literary work is integrated into a topic it becomes more real, relevant to the curriculum and, most importantly, accessible to learners.

Case study

In November 2014, the postgraduate certificate in education (PGCE) languages team at the UCL Institute of Education (IOE) was the regional winner for London in the British Academy Schools Languages Awards, with its project entitled 'London partnership launches literature'. As a PGCE team we have always been committed to, and passionate about, the teaching of culture and literature in foreign language lessons as an alternative to more transactional and instrumental approaches. With the recent changes in the NC in England, literature is on the agenda again with the aim of developing language skills.

Our strong partnership with our schools was a key element of the project. We aimed for student teachers to work in collaboration with experienced teachers and mentors in school to develop innovative ways to respond to the challenges of the new curriculum and inspire creative responses from pupils. The student teachers developed resources and approaches for integrating literature into a topic-based approach to promote language skills and cultural understanding. The languages involved were French, Spanish, German, Russian and Mandarin. The student teachers received lectures followed by a series of workshops, including ICT workshops to aid the completion of the last phase of the project.

Following an initial input, student teachers had to complete a course task as part of their second school experience between February and May 2015. The aims of the task shared with the student teachers were:

- to offer their learners an enriching and inspirational experience through working with literary texts
- to produce resources and teach using innovative activities to exploit literature and culture, in collaboration with their mentor
- to address the aspect of the KS3 NC concerned with literary texts: 'Read literary texts in the language (such as stories, songs, poems and letters), to stimulate ideas, develop creative expression and expand understanding of the language and culture' (DFE, 2013: 2).

The task consisted of seven steps completed either in school or at university at the end of the placement, as follows:

- Identify an appropriate literary text for use with a KS3 class.
- Plan a sequence of engaging target language (TL) activities (no more than a sequence of two lessons) to accompany the text and meet the

programme of study requirement. The text had to link to a topic in the scheme of work and could serve either as an introduction to the topic or as a springboard to more creative work.

- Produce a short-term plan, lessons plans and resources. Submit these to the mentor for discussion and possible development and improvement.
- Teach the lessons incorporating the literary texts, observed by the mentor and/or UCL IOE tutor. Meet with the mentor for feedback. Write up what worked well and outline areas for improvement (200 words).
- Upload their two-lesson sequence with the evaluations on Moodle (a virtual learning environment) before the end of their second school placement.
- Once at university, work in groups of three based on one element their work had in common: either the topic they taught (such as Spanish poems on the topic of clothes, French poetry and short stories on the topic of school or poetry in Spanish and German related to the topic of holidays), or the type of literary text chosen (French and Russian fairy tales, the story of Cinderella in French, French poems or Spanish poems and songs, for instance).
- In a workshop on literature and ICT, combine resources with other student teachers and create posters. Some 25 posters in A1 format were printed and presented at a literature poster conference at the end of the PGCE course; school mentors were invited and the resources shared with all the participants for future use in school.

The poster conference gave the student teachers the opportunity to present their work to their peers, tutors and subject mentors and discuss the outcomes, allowing for an exchange of ideas and experiences. The event culminated in a debate between a panel of student teachers representing different languages and university lecturers in which participants shared their opinions, reactions and the challenges they faced teaching language through literature.

Developing reading skills and linguistic proficiency

Literature can provide the stimulus and motivation to improve reading skills and develop linguistic proficiency (Ellis and Shintani, 2014), when combined with appropriate reading strategies. A scaffolded approach can be adopted to explore the literary source, using a series of steps during the teaching process. To explain the process I will adopt a theoretical framework developed by Cummins (2008), Luke and Freebody (1999) and

Scarborough (2001), who suggest three steps in the reading process: word recognition, language comprehension and text interpretation.

Word recognition

When first learning a modern foreign language it can be a challenge to move beyond the word level, phonological decoding and sight-reading (Hoover and Gough, 1990; Joshi and Aaron, 2000; McBridie-Chang and Kail, 2002; Ziegler and Goswami, 2005) and vocabulary items in isolation. There is a danger that students do not see lexis in context as part of a paragraph or a longer passage. The longer the teacher avoids the initiation to a text, the more difficult it will be for the student to gain the confidence to read and interpret the text. In this project, the PGCE student teachers demonstrated that beginner learners of a modern foreign language can access lexis in a literary context. The following example illustrates how one PGCE student teacher worked on the recognition dimension, using a French poem to revise school subjects, adjectives and time for beginners.

She started off reading the text and used one strategy for word recognition and consolidation, asking her students to stand when they recognized a word and then to repeat with her. She explained:

> While I read the poem, I asked students to stand every time they heard a school subject, time, or adjective that they knew. This really engaged them and they were keen to show me how much they knew. It also ensured that no-one was able to switch off as I read the poem aloud. I then re-read the first and last paragraphs, but this time they were listening and repeating each line after me. This, therefore, worked on their pronunciation. ... and then on their sheet they had to underline in the poem the school subjects in black, the time in blue, opinions in red and adjectives in green.

This encouraged sight-reading and decoding. She acknowledges that using a literary text as an introduction to a topic was daunting at first for the learners. However, with the right scaffolding of activities and the encouraging start her students experienced when they were able to identify the different words, she successfully achieved word recognition with them and laid the foundations for further language comprehension.

Language comprehension

Once word recognition is achieved, the next stage when reading a (literary) text is to achieve deeper comprehension. The key is to gradually move the learner to comprehension at sentence level and then at paragraph level or within a set of sentences/verses. It is only then that meaning and interpretation can start taking place and feed into the development of writing skills. To achieve comprehension of a text, the learner needs meaningful reading strategies and clear steps adopted by the teacher involving the learner actively.

One PGCE student teacher worked with a Year 8 French class on *Le Petit Nicolas* to revise and develop the past tense (see Table 4.2 for excerpts of her lesson plan, column 1 teacher activity and column 2 pupils' activity, and the different strategies used).

The first reading strategy was to invite the students to listen while she read (see Table 4.2: A1, A2): the students, in turn, read along and aloud, following the text with their finger and looking at the drawings for support (see Table 4.2: A2, B2). This type of activity facilitates a first reading, recognition and initial comprehension of words (see Table 4.2: C1, C2, D1, D2), in keeping with the final aim of discussing with their partner a summary of events in English (and eventually checking understanding with the whole class). Discussing the summary of each paragraph with a partner (see Table 4.2: F1, F2) and then eventually with the class allows the students to build their confidence in tackling long texts, as they find this approach manageable and achievable (see Table 4.2: G1, G2).

A subsequent strategy is to take the step from 'reading for gist' to reading for detail (see Table 4.2 H1, H2). This was organized through a series of oral and written activities presented in booklet format, which allowed the students to observe the forms of words, structures and tenses, and eventually tackle translation of sentences as a result of the first-reading strategy (see Table 4.2 I1, I2). The student teacher allowed the pupils to work mainly at sentence level, gradually achieving more understanding of the text at paragraph level (see Table 4.2: C2 and D2 in particular).

Text interpretation

When moving away from the text or source (Jones, 2001), what learners find most challenging is to go beyond the comprehension stage, create new meanings and eventually offer their own interpretation of the text. Kitajima (2002) proposed that computer-assisted reading materials could help learners improve their higher-order interpretation skills by embedding prompts in digital texts, enabling them to apply reading strategies. He suggests that the latter is achieved through the process of acknowledging organizational patterns within the text (Park *et al.*, 2014: 270), such as themes and word patterns. Similarly, Diamantidaki (2005, 2010) developed an online platform to understand French literature in the language classroom. This platform allows thematic access to poems and literary texts and includes built-in comprehension activities with corrections, based on the vocabulary patterns and themes that emerge from the excerpts. For the most challenging level of comprehension, the learner can choose any of the interpretations offered on the text. It is argued that choosing an interpretation reinforces one of the qualities that literary texts have, which is their polysemy. The learner is therefore not expected to find one right answer, enabling them to feel confident in their own choice of interpretation.

One PGCE student teacher worked with her Year 7 Russian class on *The Little Round Bun (Колобок)* to create and perform a script in groups, based on the story. The linguistic objectives for the lesson were to revise the topic of animals and improve speaking skills through drama. The student teacher commented on the project:

> I have high expectations of this group both in terms of level and behaviour. Presenting them with a piece of Russian text (the script from the fairy tale) would have been a daunting challenge for some of them but planning a series of activities that ensured they unpicked the text gradually, and with support if needed, actually helped to boost their confidence. Some students commented on how many words they were able to decipher without having to ask for help and this they found encouraging. Exploring a traditional piece of Russian culture made the students aware of the bigger picture and allowed them to see past the obvious tedium of getting to grips with the Cyrillic alphabet. Overall I was extremely pleased with the way the project progressed and was lucky to be able to use a third lesson to make finishing touches to scripts, spend time practising in groups their performance and then also recognizing and celebrating their efforts by filming them in class. Group performances were peer-assessed and positive feedback shared and reflected upon in books. All students gained something from this series of lessons and whenever I pass them in the corridor they now recite their lines to me. To perform their own version of a Russian fairy tale in Russian at the end of their first year of studying the language is an impressive achievement.

With these examples in mind, the following learner-friendly approach to a literary text can help guide the student through three levels of comprehension:

- Level 1: understand the basics: Who? With whom? What? Where?
- Level 2: explore the themes and images of the text.
- Level 3: guide and allow independent interpretation of meaning.

Main findings of the project

Some 62 PGCE student teachers participated in this initiative, and each submitted two lesson sequences with lesson plans and resources for French, German, Mandarin, Russian and Spanish. Figure 4.1 shows the breakdown of the different languages:

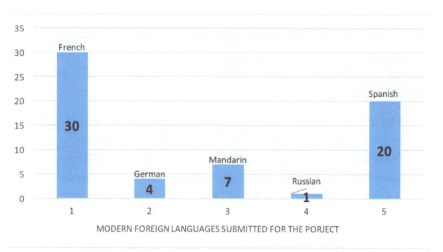

Figure 4.1: Breakdown of languages

Table 4.1 shows a selection of titles of literary extracts in the different languages the student teachers used during the project, indicating which year group they taught it to and under which topic. This illustrates the potential for the integration of literature within schemes of work.

Table 4.1: Examples of the integration of literature into topics

Language	Literary text	Topic	Year group
French	Poem: *Pour dessiner un bonhomme* by Maurice Carême	Body parts, combination of film and literature	Year 7
	Poem: *Dans Paris* by Paul Eluard	Prepositions, places in town	Year 7
	Poem: *L'écolier* by Raymond Queneau	Travel and future tense	Year 9
Spanish	Poem: *Doña Pito Piturra* by Gloria Fuertes	Items of clothing	Year 8

Language	Literary text	Topic	Year group
	Excerpt : *Diarios de Motocicleta* by Ernesto 'Che' Guevara	Travel/holidays	Year 9
German	Excerpt: *Das Tagebuch der Anne Frank* by Anne Frank Fischer	Revising past tense	Year 8
	Poem: *Er ist's* by Eduard Mörike	Creative writing	Year 9
Mandarin	Song: 我的姑娘在哪里: Where is my girl?	Revising numbers; family members; pronouns; the possessive particle 的; the adjective 好	Year 7
	Visual poem: 视觉诗 by Anatol Knotek	Understanding the concept of radicals in Chinese characters	Year 8
Russian	Traditional fairy tale: *Kolobok*	Family, animals	Year 7

Use of poems

The majority of literary texts used across languages and year groups were poems. Student teachers were presented with a set of poems during a workshop using literature in the KS3 classroom, and this may have prompted them to use poems during lessons more than any other genre.

The rationale behind this choice is based on finding texts to match the level of the students' language ability, to make literature accessible to younger learners. Poems offer brevity, clear repetitive linguistic structure and topical relevance. As one student teacher noted:

> I chose to use a Gérard de Nerval poem called *Avril* to work with a Year 7 mixed-ability group on creating some work around the topic of the seasons ... I wanted to see how literature could be used in the classroom even with younger learners ... I was generally very happy with the sequencing of activities and the way in which I scaffolded learning in order to help learners tackle such advanced French. The treasure hunt worked particularly well, with my lowest ability students managing to find the colours, while the more advanced were able to translate short sections of the poem into English.

Avril

Déjà les beaux jours, – la poussière,
Un ciel d'azur et de lumière,
Les murs enflammés, les longs soirs; -
Et rien de vert: - à peine encore
Un reflet rougeâtre décore
Les grands arbres aux rameaux noirs!
Ce beau temps me pèse et m'ennuie.
Ce n'est qu'après des jours de pluie
Que doit surgir, en un tableau,
Le printemps verdissant et rose,
Comme une nymphe fraîche éclose
Qui, souriante, sort de l'eau.

(Gérard de Nerval)

Student teachers also taught various grammatical points in context and as part of a topic in the departmental schemes of work, for example:

> I chose to teach a Paul Eluard poem called *Dans Paris* to work with a Year 7 class on revising the '*il y a*' structure on the topic of '*Dans ma chambre il y a …*':

Dans Paris

Dans Paris il y a une rue;
Dans cette rue il y a une maison;
Dans cette maison il y a un escalier;
Dans cet escalier il y a une chambre;
Dans cette chambre il y a une table;
Sur cette table il y a un tapis;
Sur ce tapis il y a une cage;
Dans cette cage il y a un nid;
Dans ce nid il y a un oeuf;
Dans cet oeuf il y a un oiseau.

L'oiseau renversa l'oeuf;
L'oeuf renversa le nid;
Le nid renversa la cage;
La cage renversa le tapis;
Le tapis renversa la table;
La table renversa la chambre;
La chambre renversa l'escalier;

> L'escalier renversa la maison;
> La maison renversa la rue;
> La rue renversa la ville de Paris.
>
> (Paul Eluard)

Thanks to the imagination that only poems can inspire, observing linguistic aspects of the language through the use of poems allowed learners to create their own versions, as one student teacher attested:

> The literature project was a really good experience for me, I really enjoyed teaching Raymond Queneau's poem *L'écolier* to my Year 9 class, as the students were all engaged. [...] The poems written by the students were amazing and show a high level of commitment. The students clapped each other when reading the poem, [which] showed me their motivation.

Another teacher, working with Spanish, observed:

> I found the poem *Doña Pito Piturra* by Gloria Fuertes [...] The second lesson was focused on the students' using their own creativity to produce a poem using the structure of the given poem. I gave them adjectives, which they had to match up with the rhyming items of clothing so that they could construct their own couplets which rhymed. Many students commented on the satisfaction of producing their own Spanish poem, which made sense and even rhymed!

Use of songs

Students got involved and got creative by making a song their own and creating their own versions. One student teacher noted:

> Students were introduced to the popular French folk/pop song *Je Veux* and gained a feeling of success through understanding its message. [...] The emphasis placed on expression and creativity led to students' producing thoughtful and creative poems of their own. Following feedback on their work, the students are going to redraft their poems and present them in an attractive way, giving them ownership over their work, and some poems will then be used as a classroom display, allowing students to take pride in their work and to feel valued.

Use of technology

The student teachers submitted all of their resources and lesson plans online (via Moodle). This allowed the tutor to observe in detail how technology was used in a lesson to enhance learning opportunities and in combination with literature. This was clearly a welcome added dimension since the first appearance of literature in the grammar translation period. PowerPoint slides and the use of attractive images such as paintings were widely used. For instance, Van Gogh's sketch of his room in Arles to his brother Theo was used as a visual aid to prompt writing: '*Dans cette chambre il y a ...*' and after introducing the poem *Dans Paris* by Paul Eluard:

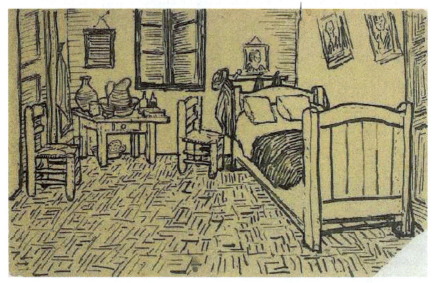

Figure 4.2: Vincent Van Gogh (1853–1890), The *Bedroom Arles*, 16 October 1888; pen and ink on paper, 13cm x 21cm. Van Gogh Museum, Amsterdam (Vincent van Gogh Foundation).

Videos were also used to work through poems, as the teacher explained: 'The correction was done through listening to the poem [*Déjeuner du Matin* by Jacques Prevert] sung by Marlene Dietrich while showing a video with pictures of Paris' key cultural sites. The students enjoyed it and had done well in the gap-fill so they could appreciate the video.'

As a creative outcome, some students combined the literature project with the film-making project and filmed pupils reciting their own creations. One PGCE student teacher commented on her work with Year 8 French pupils on the poem:

The vocabulary in the poem is very accessible with a lot of vocabulary that they have seen in previous units. The main objective of my lesson was for students to be able to study the poem and then create their own versions of an additional stanza; they will then film their versions in a later lesson.

A PGCE student teacher in Italian:

introduced *Io non ho paura*, a novel loosely based on a true story about a young boy from a wealthy family in the north of Italy who is kidnapped by a group of villagers from a fictional village in the south of Italy. The novel studies the topics of family, friendship and trust. [His] students had to act out scripted and unscripted role-plays, taking on the role of some of the characters from the novel, and were filmed doing this.

One Mandarin Chinese student teacher and member of a band created a Mandarin Chinese song to revise the topic of family, which students were filmed performing around school dressed in traditional Chinese clothing. The student teacher reported:

All pupils left the classroom inspired with ideas for the video where scenes [could] be easily improvised during shooting. Most pupils were capable of mapping their understanding of the lyrics to develop creative ideas for different scenes to be shown in the video. I was pleasantly surprised to hear that a number of pupils had actually learned the song from start to finish! Overall, this task [gave] all pupils an opportunity to ingrain the vocabulary and structures contained within the song in their long-term memory, evidencing that the project has fundamentally been very worthwhile.

Technology was used as a visual aid to motivate the students in the classroom and as a means of bringing literature alive, allowing them to make the literary text their own. Filming was an extra interactive and motivating factor along with literature, as students created their own living versions.

Use of continuous prose

PGCE student teachers also used longer texts across languages, for example: *Le Petit Nicolas* in French, an excerpt from *The Diary of Anne Frank* in German, an excerpt from *Io non ho paura* by Ammaniti Nicolo in Italian, the *Kolobok* fairy tale in Russian, the story of 拔苗助长 in Mandarin and prose in Spanish such as an extract from *Crónica de una muerte anunciada*, a novella by Gabriel García Márquez. The excerpts were used mainly to develop creative outcomes, allowing the pupils to see the language they studied in class in context and make it their own. One student teacher commented: 'I used an extract from *Crónica de una muerte anunciada* ... The outcome of this project was an extended creative writing task; students had to write their own murder mystery story in the style of the text that we had read that included all of the new vocabulary they had learned relating to the family.' Pupils' confidence in reading was increased and they learnt to report in groups and individually on longer passages: 'Many pupils commented throughout the lesson about how nice it was to have "story time" in an MFL lesson, and that they felt a sense of achievement through understanding an authentic text with their peers.'

Promoting target language culture

Using literature as a resource made the lesson meaningful and clearly related to the TL culture. Several texts were used by PGCE student teachers to make learners increasingly aware of the historical aspects of the language and culture they were studying. By doing so, learners were engaged in thoughtful debates and became increasingly interested in the language they were learning, as one student teacher reflected:

> I chose to study the short Argentinian story by Luisa Valenzuela, *De Noche Soy Tu Caballo* (*By Night I Am Your Horse*), with an Ab Initio Year 9 class. ... an upbeat lesson that was well received by both the class and class teacher. The boys seemed to be very engaged with the history side of the lesson, looking briefly into the history of dictatorships in Argentina and throughout South America. The girls, on the other hand, seemed much more in favour of the language used to describe the raw emotions of the story and the emotional effect that dictatorship and rebel fighting can have on the people left behind.

Cross- and extra-curricular links

Literary texts were also used to make links with other subjects such as English where students found the same routines followed in English reassuring. One PGCE student teacher commented: 'I have chosen the poem of G. Merveille, *Je suis en vacances* for a Year 8 class. I researched with the English department how students analyse poems in English in order to teach the concept in line with their prior knowledge.'

She therefore adopted different approaches to promote literacy, vocabulary recognition and grammatical awareness – necessary strategies that guide the learners toward an interpretation of meaning:

> The analysis of the text was very successful and students analysed the text actively using colour-coding to find verbs in different tenses and then retrieving the infinitive. This supports as well their literacy and dictionary skills. Students really enjoyed understanding the several meanings and interpretation behind the words ... Students' opinions: 'I enjoyed finding simile and stuff '; 'it was like in English so I found it easy'.

Finally, the powerful nature of a literary resource goes beyond the walls of a classroom and can inspire extra-curricular activities. The initiative shared here was very successful:

> For the literature project I taught my Year 9 Ab Initio class. The text I chose was a song by the popular artist Juanes called *La Historia de Juan (The Story of John.)* I chose this song as we had been studying the preterite tense, and this features heavily in the song. We watched a video about the plight of Colombian street children which is discussed in the song, and the students read articles on the topic and answered questions imagining they were a street child. We also planned to raise money for a charity which provides food, shelter and an education for the children.

Challenges faced and implications for future practice

The focus on literature at KS3 was enhanced on the UCL IOE PGCE Languages course thanks to this project and will remain a key element in the future. The initial response of the student teachers participating in the project showed a mixture of anticipation and trepidation around integrating the literary text, as one recalled: 'Initially the idea of using an authentic literary resource with KS3 was daunting'.

Reading through all of the lesson evaluations submitted for the project, the main challenges faced while teaching were due to:

* poor planning: 'the fill-the-gap activity was not carefully planned and it could not be completed; [...] The first one was the speed of the song (too fast and students could not entirely follow the song and pick up

the words); the second one was the length of the song (too long, and students got defeated by the challenge and gave up).'
- choice of text: 'I found that the literature project was challenging to teach. I felt that the learners were not particularly engaged with the text and did not feel confident with the tasks. It seems partly to do with the choice of text, which was perhaps too complex for the class.'
- student teachers' perceptions of challenging class behaviour: 'partly to do with the fact that they are a very challenging class who need a huge amount of support. Introducing a literary text to them and teaching it in two lessons was perhaps overambitious.'
- prescribed and demanding curriculum: 'due to the limits imposed by the schemes of work and the proximity of ... assessment,' it was not possible on some occasions to extend the project over two lessons.

Even though there were difficulties to be faced, all PGCE student teachers participated and the majority embraced the challenges successfully and, with the help of their mentors, were surprised at the overwhelmingly positive response from students:

> 'The students were motivated by the task and thoroughly enjoyed the creative nature of the second part of the lesson.'

> 'Pupils understood and responded to the poem well. They found the lesson very interesting and this is the very first time that I have seen every pupil in this class willing to participate and share ideas in the class.'

Following the conference at the end of the course and dissemination of all the resources with lesson plans to all the participants at the time, as a team we will continue to extend the dissemination of resources to the mentors in our partnership in a variety of ways: our mentor training days, exhibitions of the literature posters and presentation at conferences, for instance. The project inspired us to launch a PGCE course task, which will now remain a key element of our training year, with an annual literature poster conference to inspire and encourage our student teachers and subject mentors to experiment and innovate. The sharing of ideas and resources will serve to reinforce the UCL IOE community of practitioners, as they work together to develop their shared understandings.

Thanks to the recent changes in the NC, many school departments are in the process of adapting schemes of work and hopefully this will increasingly promote the literary element as a positive addition to a more creative and open-ended curriculum.

Questions for practice

- Where might literary texts fit most naturally into your schemes of work?
- How might you most effectively exploit these texts to develop reading skills?
- How might you most effectively exploit these texts to develop other language skills?

Further reading

Holmes, D. and Platten, D. (2005) 'Literary studies'. In Coleman, J. and Klapper, J. (eds), *Effective Learning & Teaching in Modern Languages*. Oxford: Routledge.

Pachler, N. and Allford, D. (2004) 'Literature in the communicative classroom'. In Field, K. (ed.), *Issues in Modern Foreign Languages Teaching*. London: Routledge, 223–36.

References

Collie, J. and Slater, S. (1987) *Literature in the Language Classroom*. Cambridge: CUP.

Cummins, J. (2008) 'Technology, literacy, and young second language learners: Designing educational futures'. In Parker, L.L. (ed.) *Technology-mediated Learning Environments for Young English Learners: Connections in and out of school*. New York: Lawrence Erlbaum Associates.

DfE (2013) Languages Programmes of Study: KS3. Online. www.gov. uk/government/uploads/system/uploads/attachment_data/file/239083/ SECONDARY_national_curriculum_-_Languages.pdf (accessed 10 February 2015).

Diamantidaki, F. (2005) Panorama Thématique. Online. www.panoramalitterature. com/ (accessed January 2015).

— (2010). *Internet et documents littéraires: Un moyen d'enseigner la langue*. Lille: Éditions Universitaire Européens.

Ellis, R. and Shintani, N. (2014) *Exploring Language Pedagogy Through Second Language Acquisition Research*. London: Routledge.

Hişmanoğlu, M. (2005) 'Teaching English through literature'. *Journal of Language and Linguistic Studies*, 1 (1), 53–66.

Hoover, W.A. and Gough, P.B. (1990) 'The simple view of reading'. *Reading and Writing*, 2 (2), 127–60.

Jones, B. (2001) *Developing Learning Strategies: Advanced pathfinder 2*. London: CILT.

Joshi, R.M. and Aaron, P.G. (2000) 'The component model of reading: Simple view of reading made a little more complex'. *Reading Psychology*, 21 (2), 85–97.

Kitajima, R. (2002) 'Enhancing higher order interpretation skills for Japanese reading'. *CALICO Journal*, 19 (3), 571–81.

Luke, A. and Freebody, P. (1999) 'A map of possible practices: Further notes on the four resources model'. *Practically Primary*, 4 (2), 5–8.

MacKay, S. (1982) 'Literature in the ESL classroom'. *TESOL Quarterly,* 16 (4), 529.

McBride-Chang, C. and Kail, R.V. (2002) 'Cross-cultural similarities in the predictors of reading acquisition'. *Child Development,* 73 (5), 392–407.

Mitchell, K.R. (2008) *Intention and Text: Towards an intentionality of literary form.* London: Continuum International Publishing Group.

Morrow, K. (1979) 'Communicative language testing: Revolution or evolution?'. In Brumfit, C. and Johnson, K. (eds), *The Communicative Approach to Language Teaching.* Oxford: Oxford University Press.

Park, Y., Zheng, B., Lawrence, J. and Warschauer, M. (2014) 'Technology-enhanced reading environments'. In Thomas, M., Reinders, H. and Warschauer, M. (eds), *Contemporary Computer-Assisted Language Learning.* London: Bloomsbury.

Scarborough, H. (2001) 'Connecting early language and literacy to later reading (dis) abilities'. In Neuman, S.B. and Dickinson, D.K. (eds), *Handbook of Early Literacy Research.* New York: Guilford.

Thom Thom, N.T. (2008) 'Using literary texts in language teaching'. *VNU Journal of Science, Foreign Languages* 24, 120–26. Online. http://tapchi.vnu.edu.vn/2_208_NN/6.pdf (accessed 3 July 2016).

Widdowson, H.G. (2003) *Defining Issues in English Language Teaching.* Oxford: Oxford University Press.

Ziegler, J.C. and Goswami, U. (2005). 'Reading acquisition, developmental dyslexia, and skilled reading across languages: A psycholinguistic grain size theory'. *Psychological Bulletin,* 131 (1), 3–29.

References of literary sources presented in this chapter

Carême, M. *Pour dessiner un bonhomme.* Online. www.ecole-mairie-jassans.org/photos/classes/serge/poesies.pdf (accessed 3 July 2016).

Eluard, P. *Dans Paris.* www.leflux.fr/content/exercice-1 (accessed 3 July 2016).

Frank, A.M. (1947) *Das Tagebuch der Anne Frank.* Frankfurt am Main: Fischer Taschenbuch Verlag GmbH.

Fuertes, G. *Doña Pito Piturra.* Online. www.poeticous.com/gloria-fuertes/dona-pitu-piturra?locale=en (accessed 3 July 2016).

Goscinny, R. and Sempé, J.J. (1960) *Le Petit Nicholas.* Paris: Denoël.

Guevara, E. (1995) *Diarios de Motocicleta.* New York: Ocean Press.

Knotek, A. 视觉诗. Online. http://th.weibo.com/user/2941981341/3837459505299 154 (accessed 4 May 2015).

Kolobok, Russian fairy tale. Online. http://feb-web.ru/feb/skazki/texts/af0/af1/af1-0462.htm (accessed 4 May 2015).

Marquez, G.G. (1982) *Crónica de una muerte anunciada.* Bruguera: Narradores de Hoy.

Mörike, E. *Er ist's.* Online. www.lyrikwelt.de/gedichte/moerikeg3.htm (accessed 10 April 2015).

Nerval, G. *Avril.* Online. http://ekladata.com/7gY9QCbgOktz1mbWYc6SPGwVZXk.jpg (accessed 10 April 2015).

Nicolo, A. (2001) Io no ho paura. Torino: Giulio Einaudi Editore.

Prevert, J. Online. https://vivelapoesie.wordpress.com/2013/07/09/dejeuner-du-matin/ (accessed February 2015).

Queneau, R. *L'écolier*. Online. www.poetica.fr/poeme-844/raymond-queneau-ecolier (accessed 10 April 2015).

Van Gogh, V. *Bedroom in Arles*. Online. https://en.wikipedia.org/wiki/Bedroom_in_Arles (accessed 4 May 2015).

Webster, C. 我的姑娘在哪里, original composer of the song, PGCE Languages UCL IOE student 2014–2015.

Appendix

Table 4.2: Excerpts of Year 8 lesson plan teaching from *Le Petit Nicolas*

Teacher activity	Pupil activity
A1 Invite pupils to gather round and listen to the teacher read the story. Instruct pupils to follow the text through with their finger.	A2 Pupils offer the names of the writer (René Goscinny) and the illustrator (Jean-Jacques Sempé) and look through the illustrations in the short story first.
B1 Elicit the meaning of 'un carnet' in English. Use descriptive language and mime to support TL. *Un carnet, c'est 'a parent/ teacher contact book'/'report book' en anglais.*	B2 Pupils discuss the meaning of the noun 'carnet' from the drawings and talk to their partner about what the English noun would be. A pupil shares the correct translation: *'a parent/teacher contact book, a report book'.*
C1 Read the story. Use mime, different voices and gesture to support the learning. Stop occasionally to elicit the next sentence(s) from pupils. Stop after each paragraph to elicit a summary of events in English from a variety of pupils to ensure they are following the text and working together to understand the gist.	C2 Pupils read along and read aloud through the short story, following the text with their finger. They look at the drawings for support and stop at the end of every long paragraph to check understanding through a quick chat with their partner and a summary of the events in English with the whole class.

D1

At the end of the story, nominate pupils to ask for their opinion of the short story – what they liked and disliked in terms of plot, characters and setting etc.

D2

At the end of the story, pupils share their thoughts and their likes and dislikes about the plot and characters etc.

E1

Graded worksheet. Instruct pupils to work in pairs. Give instructions for completion of the activities up to, and including, the reading comprehension (Gold 2) activity. Nominate to elicit the English translation of instructions, to check comprehension.

E2

Pupils listen to the instructions and participate in the modelled examples for each activity. Pupils identify levels of challenge and nominated pupils give the English translation of the instructions to check and clarify meaning has been understood by all.

F1

Circulate to monitor. Give support and praise. Remind pupils of the 3Bs (brain, book, buddy) and reinforce the school policy of offering choice and challenge to promote independent and peer learning. Rearrange seating if necessary to enhance the Zone of Proximal Development (ZPD) for these activities and monitor pairs throughout.

F2

Pupils work in pairs to support each other through the activities. All will complete the Bronze and most of the Silver; some will complete the gold activities; and very few will potentially start on the Gold Star challenge of identifying the past tense examples in the text.

G1

Whole-class feedback up to the end of the reading comprehension (Gold 2). Board vocabulary and show the extension responses without elicitation.

G2

Nominated pupils give the answers to the activities up to, and including, the reading comprehension. All pupils self-assess their work by looking at the visual feedback on the PowerPoint slides to support all oral feedback.

H1

Refer pupils back to the success criteria and ask them to identify the level of success they feel they have attained in today's lesson. Ask pupils to talk to their partner and identify what new skills they feel they have learnt today when reading an extended passage of text in French.

H2

Pupils refer back to the success criteria and identify the level of success they feel they have confidently attained for today's lesson. Pupils share with each other what new skills they feel they have learned today – reading for gist and reading for detail.

I1

Take questions from the pupils and board further examples of new language. Nominated pupils to manipulate and translate these words and phrases. Drill pronunciation chorally and individually at appropriate points.

I2

Pupils ask questions about the activities and copy down the examples of new language from the whiteboard. Pupils participate in, and respond to, the elicitation of synonyms, antonyms, manipulation at sentence level and in terms of translations. Pupils drill language chorally and individually.

Chapter 5

Teaching literature to promote creativity in language learning

Simon Coffey

The creativity craze

Creativity has become something of a buzzword in recent years, as testified by the increasing use of the term across a range of educational discourses. The concept has now appeared in the *National Curriculum for Languages* for the first time, in the statement, 'Pupils should be taught to ... develop creative expression' (DFE, 2013: 2), and a number of publications foreground creativity in language teaching. Recent research has shown there is some diversity around how teachers understand creativity. For instance, Coffey and Leung (2015) found that some teachers talk about creativity as an intrinsic personal quality while others see it as a professional skill that can be acquired, although both perceptions in Coffey and Leung's study were seen as improving student engagement through 'thinking outside of the box':

> We see therefore that, where the teacher self-identifies as a creative *type* (artist, writer etc.), creativity can be understood as a natural resource that resides in them and that they can tap into for their teaching. In contrast, other teachers associate creativity as a professional attribute, or skill, to be developed, requiring and displaying effort. For some, the teacher is the primary agent of classroom creativity while for others students can be encouraged to develop creative strategies to take greater ownership of their learning.
>
> (Coffey and Leung, 2015: 123)

Furthermore, when asked what they understand creativity to mean in their classrooms, some teachers focused on *creative language* (which they defined as literary or poetic) while others spoke about *creative pedagogy*, that is, presenting traditional (communicative, formulaic) language but through innovative and engaging pedagogic techniques. The first impression is founded on the idea that there is a difference between creative and non-creative language where creative is equated with literary forms. As Carter points out, though, 'creativity is pervasive in language use: in idioms and everyday metaphor; in jokes; in advertising and newspaper headlines; and in the highly patterned instances of literary texts' (Carter, 1996: 1). Tannen also comments that 'ordinary conversation is made up of linguistic strategies that have been thought quintessentially literary' (Tannen, 1989: 1). These creative linguistic strategies (which might include alliteration, metaphor, rhythm and so on) feature in naturally occurring interactions.

The traditional study of literariness in literary criticism has looked for formal distinguishing properties but, more recently, scholars have recognized the push and pull between originality and creativity, on the one hand, and standardized, regulated language, on the other. While acknowledging that everyday interaction is indeed creative, Hall adds that, at the same time, everyday interaction also consists largely of 'pre-fabricated' language, and he compares linguistic creativity and what he calls 'formulaicity' in language. He suggests that 'the way in which these apparently contradictory findings can be reconciled is to see linguistic creativity, in life as in writing, as a constrained activity, very real, but operating within constraints' (Hall, 2005: 33).

Sometimes creative wordplay is conscious – indeed McRae (1991) used the term 'literature with a small "l"' to denote puns and other forms of verbal artistry for humorous or dramatic effect in mundane language – but often it is instinctive. In either case, one undeveloped aspect of language pedagogy is the exploration of what Jakobson and Waugh (1979) famously called the 'sound shapes' of words. Such wordplay can be explored through memorizing and enjoying forms that have been marginalized by communicative syllabuses as unnatural and/or unnecessary. To give one example of such wordplay, spoonerisms, which provide such delightful lines as *aimable souvent est sable mouvant*, constitute a highly regarded poetic form in French (see Étienne's 1957 classic work on *la contrepèterie*).

In terms of cognitive measures, creativity – or rather creative thinking – is usually defined as 'divergent thinking', and we have known for a long time that, following this definition, bilingual students show greater creativity. Little research has been done on the creative potential of students learning a foreign language in a formal context such as the classroom. However, some classroom-based research that has been carried out concludes that learning foreign languages (FLs) to a higher level does, indeed, enhance divergent thinking abilities (Ghonsooly and Showqi, 2012).

Literature back in vogue

In modern foreign languages (MFL) lessons in English schools, literature has long been the preserve of the relatively small number of students who study a language at A-level, and when set texts were cut from post-16 MFL syllabus there was some coverage in the media fearing a loss of the cultural dimension to language learning and a dumbing-down of language competence to a narrow skills focus. The separation between 'literature' and 'language' became especially salient in the wake of the introduction of the GCSE in 1986 and then the National Curriculum (NC) for languages in 1992. This saw the promotion and enactment in the English MFL curriculum of the prevalent dogma of communicative language teaching, confirming the 'dominant contemporary assumption ... that the purpose of foreign language teaching is to develop communicative competence' (Byram, 2010: 317).

The traditional separation of language and literature is a divide deeply embedded in the UK education system between language-as-a-skill and literature-as-content. This divide seems to me something of a false dichotomy, as the nuts and bolts of language work (grammar, lexis, syntax) can be achieved through the exploitation of literary texts just as much as through newspaper articles or sound recordings of interactional language. There are indeed some definitional parameters defining what counts as literature – and I consider these next – but these parameters are porous rather than rigid and often imposed by cultural mechanisms rather than rigorous linguistic analysis. As mentioned above, everyday language can equally be described as poetic and aesthetically pleasing (or not) and daily interactions are replete with rhetorical devices.

More recently, the horizons for language learning have been broadened in the context of two key developments, both resulting, in part, from the perceived 'language crisis' as fewer British students choose to study languages beyond post-compulsory phases. First, the instrumentalist assumption that the a priori goal of language learning is communicative competence, understood as language for transactional purposes, is recognized as increasingly inadequate given the overwhelming dominance of English use in tourism and service encounters. I would add here that the goal of communicative competence has never, in any event, fully translated into MFL pedagogic practice. Second, the social turn in applied linguistics has extended the project of language learning from a narrow conception of skills development through drill-and-practice toward a recognition that engaging with language learning entails an engagement in socially and historically situated resources that are both linguistic and cultural. The current repositioning acknowledges the traditional (pre-communicative dogma) rich heritage of language learning as a scholarly activity within humanistic intellectual arts.

The shift in wording of the NC illustrates this change of emphasis. In the 2004 version of the NC we see that:

> Pupils should be taught techniques for skimming and for scanning written texts for information ... [and] ... how to summarise and report the main points of spoken or written texts, using notes where appropriate.
>
> (QCA, 2004: 108)

Here we see the focus on retrieving the informational content of a text, which is so characteristic of the communicative approach. In the 2007 version of the NC we see that guidance is modified to state that:

> Pupils should be taught to use a range of resources, including ICT, for accessing and communicating information in the target language ... [and to] ... listen to, read or view a range of materials, including authentic materials in the target language, both to support learning and for personal interest and enjoyment.
>
> (QCA, 2007: 169)

The key change here is the inclusion of the words *personal interest* and *enjoyment*, a move which signals acknowledgement of the need for personal investment in language learning rather than positioning the student as a mechanical language processor. However, the type of texts suggested, although 'authentic', still implies that they have informational content to process within the communicative paradigm. In the most recent version of the *National Curriculum in England: Language programmes of study* there is explicit reference to using literary texts:

> (KS2) Pupils should be taught to appreciate stories, songs, poems and rhymes in the language.

> (KS3) Pupils should be taught to read literary texts in the language [such as stories, songs, poems and letters] to stimulate ideas, develop creative expression and expand understanding of the language and culture.
>
> (DfE, 2013: 2)

This is quite a shift, as we see literary texts included for the first time in the NC for languages alongside the ubiquitous *mot de jour* 'creative'. We see here a loosening of the communicative imperative to allow space for personal engagement with language for *pleasure* and the development of *creativity* and *cultural understanding*. At post-16, the planned reforms to A-level (effective from September 2016 for languages) will require students to study at least one literary text, defined as a 'piece of fiction or drama or life writing or collection of poetry' (A-Level Content Advisery Board, 2014: 4). In the next section I present some arguments in favour of using literature in language lessons, and then present an example of what this can look like.

Defining literary texts

The characteristics of literature for pedagogic purposes have been distinguished by different authors, and the question of what constitutes a literary text is not straightforward. Among the many alternatives, I like Carter's description of literary discourse as 'culturally-rooted language which is purposefully patterned and representational, which actively promotes a process of interpretation and which encourages a pleasurable interaction with and negotiation of its meanings' (Carter, 1996: 12).

Carter emphasizes here the three characteristics that I find it useful to include as an analytical lens when looking at literature for pedagogic purposes, namely, literary text as:

- an authentic model of language
- a cultural artefact
- a resource for studying the aesthetic dimension of language.

The three characteristics I have identified are intended to be *arguments for* using literary texts in the classroom. At the same time, through my discussion, I invite the reader to think about *how* these can guide teachers in deciding what type of text could work best for their students, given their age and range of interests.

An authentic model of language

Literary texts are authentic in the sense that they are artefacts produced for consumption by native speakers (notwithstanding the definitional problems around this term) rather than specifically produced for language learners. In this respect, as a model of language, literary texts can be compared to the authentic resources advocated in a more communicative-oriented syllabus. One difference, however, is that a literary text does not present itself as necessarily replicable in a real-life communicative situation (such as menu items or formulaic email phrases).

The length of text is likely to be a deciding factor in choosing which text is appropriate to use and we might distinguish between text and extract, where '*text* ... is a number of sentences bound together by cohesive ties, and giving meaning to each other. *Extract* may be regarded as part of a text, artificially separated for purposes of quotation or study from other sentences, with which, to a greater or lesser extent, it coheres' (Cook, 1986: 152). As Cook points out, the notion of text is semantic rather than grammatical: 'A single sentence is always a complete grammatical unit; it is seldom semantically complete' (ibid.). So, if a teacher wishes to extract part of a text for exploitation in the classroom, some thought needs to be given to the cohesion of the extract when separated from its intended whole. Furthermore, as with all 'authentic' models of language, whether a shopping list or a poem, teachers need to make decisions about how to frame the text to achieve sound pedagogical aims.

A cultural artefact

Intercultural learning is a key (if not *the* key) rationale for foreign language learning where instrumental purposes are not apparent, as is the case for many learners of MFL in the UK, given the worldwide currency of English. It is useful to distinguish between the concept of intercultural competence and learning cultural knowledge. The latter has traditionally been the aim of learning the literary cultural canon of a prestigious language (French, German, Russian and so on.). The more recent formulation posits a model of 'intercultural competence (that) involves an awareness of difference and a consequent reflection on one's own culturally specific socialisation and limitations' (Byram *et al.*, 1994: 152). Developing intercultural competence from this perspective privileges language students' potential to understand language as symbolic of a range of interpersonal meanings. Given this model, language learning offers to support the 'growth of a ... sense of symbolic self' (Kramsch, 2006: 199).

In other words, rather than studying a textual artefact for cultural 'knowledge' it is more helpful to think in terms of developing cultural awareness or sensitivity. Knowledge can connote a rather static body of facts about a culture, which risks reductively learning about how *they* do things in *that* language, rather than developing a reflexive sensitivity to how language and culture are mutually constitutive and always in process. This emphasis helps us to see literary texts not just as cultural icons, but also as being the product of situated moments in the cultural history of a language and society.

Studying the aesthetic dimension of language

This criterion is arguably the most problematic and straddles both the view of a literary text as an authentic model of language and as a cultural artefact. In arguing the point that language is more than its message, Hawkes states that poetic language is:

> deliberately self-conscious, self-aware. It emphasises itself as a 'medium' over and above the 'message' it contains; ... as a result, words in poetry have the status of not simply vehicles for thoughts, but of objects in their own right, autonomous concrete entities.
>
> (Hawkes, 1977: 63–4)

The effect of the language will be determined by strategies such as the speed at which the text is read and the emphasis given to particular sounds. To exemplify this point, Pickett cites some lines from Auden ('Lay your sleeping head, my love, Human on my faithless arm ...') to illustrate how language structures carry their own form and rhythm that are so strongly patterned that they remain as 'semantic residue' carried in the head 'like an empty bucket in search of water' (Pickett, 1986: 279). We are all familiar with the rhythm of sounds from songs and particularly striking forms of speech which echo in our minds over and beyond the referential content of the words.

Although Pickett is referring specifically to poetic language per se, I would argue that this poetic potential can be extended to any literary text, as defined by Carter (1996), and possibly to non-literary language forms as well. Here we are dealing with the aesthetics of language, the argument being that language forms can never be wholly dissociated from their aesthetic value, 'that there are indeed real correspondences between forms and meanings in a language' (Hall, 2005: 245). This aesthetic dimension is referred to in literary criticism as iconicity, defined by Hall as 'the relation of the sound or shape of words to the meanings they have. [This relation is] known only subconsciously by native speakers, but recognised when exploited by literary writers or advertisers, and ... should be drawn to the attention of the language learner' (ibid.).

As an example of this focus on wordplay, on the lexical level, we can refer to a recent project promoted by the Institut Français de Londres. The project is called *Dis-moi dix mots*, the title of which already carries a poetic quality through its alliteration and rhythm. The objective of the project, initiated by the French Ministry of Culture and Communication, is to focus on ten words in French grouped under a theme, and to create an artistic piece of work inspired by these words. The winning entries are currently (2016) being exhibited at the Tate and include first-prize winners Reay Primary School from London. *Dis-moi dix mots* is a striking initiative in which artistic representation unites both referential meaning and the sound shape of words. In the next section I illustrate how a literary text can be used in a French class with a Year 7 group. Further information can be found at www.institut-francais.org.uk/news-education/the-concours-des-10-mots-in-partnership-with-the-tate/.

Case study

The module presented in this chapter as an example of using literature to promote creativity (see Table 5.1) was taught by Audrey who teaches MFL at a boys' school near London. Two years after completing her PGCE in MFL at King's College London, Audrey returned to King's to take her MA in MFL Education. For her MA dissertation she wrote a detailed account of a sequence she taught to a Year 7 group using literature within a 'content and language integrated learning' (CLIL) framework (Coyle *et al.*, 2010).

There is clearly overlap between planning for CLIL and planning for using literary texts in the MFL classroom, in particular with regard to balancing learning aims between form (language) and content (new informational input). However, CLIL defines new content as covering other areas of the curriculum (science, history and so on), and I wish to focus here on the unique contribution of combining language–literary study in its own right to stimulate engagement and intellectual development. Unlike some writers on CLIL, I do not see that linguistic knowledge is, at least in MFL, separable from content knowledge, although this distinction can serve as a planning tool and, as Audrey noted in her dissertation:

> teachers could alternate between a greater focus on form or on subject content, which would be reflected in their choice of resources as well as in the learning objectives of their lessons. This approach would allow students not to focus on both content and form simultaneously, which could also impact positively on their level of motivation.

For the purposes of her dissertation, Audrey framed her teaching sequence as a research project with a detailed, reflexive account of her decision-making throughout the process and she collected student feedback to respond to her research questions focusing on student engagement and motivation. While she has kindly given me permission to reproduce extracts of her dissertation here, the manner in which Audrey's work is represented in this chapter is entirely attributable to me and I carry the whole responsibility for any oversights or gaps. Audrey chose to use a literary text because, in her words:

Extract 1

Using a book also generated a sense of expectation in students; they were eager to discover what was going to happen to the main characters. This impacted positively on their willingness to cope with more unknown language, as they wanted to follow the storylines. What appealed even more to students than understanding the story itself was understanding the characters. They attributed feelings and emotions to specific characters which supported their understanding of the story as a whole ... [one student said after the sequence]: 'you grew to people like the little prince but you didn't really grow on the banker person because he was not very friendly and just gave simple answers'.

The text she chose was *Le Petit Prince* by Antoine de Saint-Exupéry, first published in 1943 and the most widely translated French book. Audrey says the following about her choice of book:

Extract 2

My aim was for the boys to be captivated by the story and to want to read more. I therefore liaised with our librarian and asked her what kind of books Year 7 students tend to borrow. Her answer was adventure books. I initially selected *Vingt mille lieues sous les mers* by Jules Verne as it is an adventure story which involves fictional elements such as the 'Nautilus' ship. When I started to reflect on the main objectives of my unit of work, I soon realised that what I truly wanted my students to be able to do was on two different levels: firstly I wanted them to understand the plot of the story and to be able to describe it in their own words, but secondly and more importantly, I wanted them to interpret the meaning of the story, to look for hidden messages and to read in between the lines. My choice of *Vingt mille lieues sous les mers* did not really allow me to interpret the story as it is mainly a succession of adventures. I then selected *Le Petit Prince* because it is, in fact, a philosophical tale, which is quirky and provides ample scope for interpretation as well as description. The language of the book is quite simple as it is repetitive at times, and a lot of original illustrations are included in the book, which support students' understanding. As I intended to work on the book for four weeks, I had to select specific chapters of the book depending on their length and their role in the overall story. What was also key to my selection was the chapters' potential in terms of types of activities which could be created. For example, I chose Chapters 11 and 13 as they respectively describe the meeting of the *Petit Prince* with the conceited man and the businessman. These two chapters are mainly composed of dialogues, which my students could act out to practise their pronunciation and intonation. Once I had selected the chapters, I simplified the language of each chapter, for example the whole story is narrated in the past tense and I wanted my students to be able to work mainly on the present tense. In this case I had to be flexible when establishing linguistic objectives because the text under study dictates them.

In short, *Le Petit Prince* was considered especially suitable for several reasons: the language is relatively simple; there is rhythmic repetition; there are attractive illustrations to accompany the text; and the selected chapters featured dialogue that offered the potential to act out the language. Audrey taught 13 lessons of 40 minutes across a period of four weeks. As well as framing the sequence as a research project for her MA dissertation, Audrey integrated the sequence into the career plan development required by the school/department, and a colleague observed her teaching and gave informal feedback. An overview of the sequence (Unit of Work) is included as an appendix. In her planning, Audrey considered carefully the balance between content and form. I think this offers a useful binary model which incorporates perennial issues in MFL planning such as target language (TL) use and the balance between receptive and productive language development.

Content vs form

There is always an intuitive balance between encouraging creativity and meeting the constraints of structural language work. In this respect, Audrey was pragmatic and used English to confirm conceptual understanding:

Extract 3

[Given that] students are working on more cognitively demanding material, production skills such as writing and speaking in particular take more time to develop. Students needed some time to adapt to the type of activities they had to do on *Le Petit Prince* and it would have been counterproductive to require them to use the target language to communicate. ... Swain and Lapkin (2005) consider [the mother tongue in the language classroom] as a regulator, which enables students to internalise the target language fully. Allowing students to discuss the storylines of the book in English in the first place supported their understanding and contributed to a positive learning environment. Sakari Roiha (2014) even compares the mother tongue to a differentiation tool as it contributes to supporting lower-ability students. In a later phase, students were initially asked to produce written answers in the target language and then orally as a class discussion.

Not wishing to cognitively overload her students, Audrey, as she states in Extract 2, adapted the text. This involved selecting parts of the whole text (convenient with this work given that there are a number of more or less self-contained chapters) and changing past tenses to the present. The complexity of using authentic texts is a challenge, especially for younger learners. If the challenge is too great and the:

work is perceived to be too difficult, pupils will feel that they are not up to the task. This may be because the task does not build on the frame of knowledge and skills that has previously been developed, or it may be that the task has not been "scaffolded" adequately with support material, further explanation or other sources of support.

(Coffey, 2011: 199).

As Audrey states:

Extract 4

Spending time making a resource attractive with visual aids supports students' learning and contributes to a positive affective reaction. Another question which is key to using literature, in my case, is whether to adapt the language level of the original text or to use the text in its authentic form. Sharples (1999) explains that the author's writing style reflects the world in which he/she lives and impacts on the language used. As a consequence, modifying a text would mean losing some of its cultural and social content. On the other hand, Maun (2006) calls for a redefinition of authenticity and states that a text is authentic as long as the intended audience reads it, but in the classroom, the language learner is not the intended reader, which justifies adapting the original text. Besides, adapting a text according to the language level of specific students does not necessarily mean that the cultural and social references are lost if the teacher is aware of them and subsequently analyses them in his or her teaching sequence.

At the end of the sequence Audrey distributed questionnaires to all students in the Year 7 group and then conducted short interviews (5–10 minutes) during a lunch-time, with three targeted students, selected to reflect contrasting levels of confidence or ability in French. The interview scripts revealed that the students had found the prospect of reading a book in French daunting but had engaged positively with it (as Audrey describes in Extract 1). One student told her: 'I've never actually read a French book before so it was quite cool for me'.

Extract 5

[The] ability to empathise with the characters of the story ... reflects the cultural dimension of the book. The adjective 'different' was used repeatedly to describe the lessons, which shows that students identified a different teaching style and they had to work differently themselves. For example, they had to use learning strategies much more to complete challenging activities and were working in groups on a regular basis.

Not only do the exchanges between the prince and the various characters he encounters provide linguistic and intercultural learning opportunities, but also the narrative is intrinsically about ethical development as the characters he meets can be conceited or greedy, as in the case of the businessman from Chapter 11 of *Le Petit Prince* (illustrated in Figure 5.1) who claims ownership of the stars as he counts them.

- Et moi je possède les étoiles, puisque jamais personne avant moi n'a pensé à les posséder.
- Ça c'est vrai, dit le petit prince. Et qu'en fais-tu?
- Je les gère. Je les compte et je les recompte, dit le businessman. C'est difficile. Mais je suis un homme sérieux!

Figure 5.1: The businessman in *Le Petit Prince*

Discussion and conclusion

Audrey's taught sequence focused on language structure and introducing French literature as a genre to discuss engaging content. Her use of literature demonstrates what Carter (1996: 2) describes as a 'language-based' approach, whereby she integrated language and literature study. This is the model that secondary schools mostly use, although it is mainly associated with more advanced learners and has only recently (in the UK) been re-introduced for learners at earlier stages. However, it is worth mentioning that other treatments of literature in the classroom are also available, which Carter calls 'stylistic approaches' (ibid.: see also Widdowson, 1975). This category might include poetry or other language forms where the focus is on the language itself rather than content, such as the aforementioned *Dis-moi dix mots* project. This approach may typically be seen with more advanced learners (university students) or early learners in primary school. Wordplay is deployed frequently with younger children, as in the case of the primary school teacher of German (cited in Jones and Coffey, 2013) who uses different forms of onomatopoeia and rhymes – such as *lecker* and *igitt-igitt* (meaning 'yummy' and 'yuck') – to great effect. The same teacher also recounts how she teaches Year 2 (6–7 year olds) the story of *Sleeping Beauty* (*Dornröschen*) by playing on the sound shape of certain words:

> The children love the word '*böse*' as in '*die böse Fee*', the wicked fairy who casts the terrible spell on Dornröschen. It can be said in a very nasty way, and a lot of fun can be had with one half of the class chanting *Die böse Fee!*, while the other half responds *Die gute Fee*, with a totally different expression.
>
> (cited in Jones and Coffey, 2013: 50)

As well as the usual language class work of grammar, syntax and lexis, literary texts can also, I claim, motivate because both narrative and aesthetics engage learners on an emotional level, drawing them in. Audrey's sequence corroborates other initiatives where combining text and image in narrative has achieved greater engagement with foreign language learning. This can be seen, for instance, in Norton and Vanderheyden's (2004) study of adolescent learners using comics to learn English, in which learners valued the accessibility of the stories (text supported by illustrations) and the insights into Canadian culture as well as engaging with language.

One of Audrey's students told her that acting out language (reading out in role) is interesting 'because if you have emotions to it, if you don't understand the words, you can still see what's kind of happening, it helps how people react to it'. This is a clear acknowledgement from a Year 7 student that emotional investment through voice and pitch carry meaning beyond the informational content of language. The explicit mention of emotional investment in the classroom and the recognition that language use is inherently affective both point to important mechanisms for broadening linguistic understanding in students and developing empathy through narrative work. The development of empathy – the key rationale underpinning intercultural competence – is closely related to enjoyment of narrative. As Kümmerling-Meibauer (2014: 68) reports, many scholars have investigated why 'people enjoy reading fiction and to what extent this is connected with identifying with characters' (see also Zunshine, 2006). Audrey found that this was a principal theme from her feedback data. Kümmerling-Meibauer refers to:

> the delight readers might gain from recognising themselves or real people they know in the characters' states of mind. Even if (readers) realise that these characters reveal somewhat strange or unusual—perhaps even disgusting—feelings, ideas, and behaviour, they nevertheless might get insights into states of mind that they usually would not encounter in their immediate surroundings.
>
> (ibid.)

Using stories is therefore intrinsically motivating, and work with literary texts can function on many different levels. As a language model, this approach provides a motivating text which draws readers in through plot and characters. Children enjoy the rhythm and repetition that typically characterize children's stories, including traditional tales, while the musicality of rhythmic repetition reinforces linguistic forms and has been shown to increase memory retention in language learning (Legg, 2009). As a cultural artefact, characterization in literary texts offers the potential to develop empathy (intercultural competence) through the exploration of other people's emotionally-invested identity positions and choices. Literature also encourages consideration of the tension between universality and cultural specificity when exploring themes such as the pathos of the pointless materialism of the businessman in *Le Petit Prince*.

Finally, the use of literature encourages a creative, playful (Coffey, 2014) vision of language, offering the potential to exploit the aesthetic dimension of language through drawing and acting out. The implications of using literary texts are therefore far-reaching, as both students and teachers extend our notions of language beyond a naive conception of a medium for transactional communication toward the exploration of new narrative worlds that unfold, while enjoying the sound shapes of new words.

Questions for practice

- How are stories used – or how could they be used – in your MFL teaching context and with different age groups? (This can include graphic novels, poems, film scripts, and short stories as well as novels.)
- Once you have decided on a suitable text, what elements can be exploited (characters, setting, plotline) and how can the text be rendered into accessible language for your students?
- How can you encourage students to engage with the different sound shapes of words and phonological rhythms of the languages you teach (such as by using song, rhyme or onomatopoeia)?
- What are the broader cultural and citizenship dimensions that can be exploited through using a literary text?
- What cross-curricular skills (such as drawing, acting out, music) can be developed to broaden the sensory and aesthetic appreciation of language?

Further reading

Carter, R. and McRae, J. (eds) (1996) *Language, Literature and the Learner: Creative classroom practice*. London and New York, NY: Routledge.
Hall, G. (2005) *Literature in Language Education*. New York: Palgrave Macmillan.
Richards, J. and Jones, R. (eds) (2015) *Creativity and Language Teaching: Perspectives from research and practice*. London: Routledge.

References

A-Level Content Advisery Board (2014) *Modern Languages, A Level and AS Level Illustrative Content: Themes, works and topics for individual projects.* Online. https://alevelcontent.files.wordpress.com/2014/12/alcab-revised-mfl-indicative-lists-december-2014.pdf (accessed 31 May 2015).

Byram, M. (2010) 'Linguistic and cultural education for "Bildung" and citizenship'. *Modern Language Journal*, 94 (2), 317–21.

Byram, M., Morgan, C. and Colleagues (1994) *Teaching-and-Learning-Language-and-Culture.* Clevedon: Multilingual Matters.

Carter, R. (1996) 'Look both ways before crossing: Developments in the language and literature classroom'. In Carter, R. and McRae, J. (eds), *Language, Literature and the Learner: Creative classroom practice.* London and New York, NY: Routledge.

Carter, R. and McRae, J. (eds) (1996) *Language, Literature and the Learner: Creative classroom practice.* London and New York, NY: Routledge.

Coffey, S. (2011) 'Differentiation in theory and practice'. In Dillon, J. and Maguire, M. (eds), *Becoming a Teacher,* 4th edn. Milton Keynes: Open University Press.

— (2014) 'Language learning and making the mundane special'. In Baider, F. and Cislaru, G. (eds), *Linguistic Approaches to Emotion in Context.* Amsterdam: John Benjamins.

Coffey, S. and Leung, C. (2015) 'Creativity in language teaching: Voices from the classroom'. In Richards, J. and Jones, R. (eds), *Creativity and Language Teaching: Perspectives from research and practice.* London: Routledge.

Cook, G. (1986) 'Texts, extracts and stylistic texture'. In Brumfit, C. and Carter, R. (eds), *Literature and Language Teaching.* Oxford: Oxford University Press.

Coyle, D., Hood, P. and Marsh, D. (2010) *CLIL: Content and language integrated learning.* Cambridge: CUP.

DfE (2013) *National Curriculum in England: Languages programmes of study.* Online. www.gov.uk/government/publications/national-curriculum-in-england-languages-progammes-of-study/national-curriculum-in-england-languages-progammes-of-study (accessed 1 August 2015).

Étienne, L. (1957) *L'Art du Contrepet: Petit traité à l'usage des amateurs pour résoudre les contrepèteries proposées et en inventer de nouvelles.* Paris: J.-J. Pauvert.

Ghonsooly, B. and Showqi, S. (2012) 'The effects of foreign language learning on creativity'. *English Language Teaching*, 5 (4). Online. www.ccsenet.org/journal/index.php/elt/article/view/15947/10712 (accessed 3 July 2016).

Hall, G. (2005) *Literature in Language Education.* New York: Palgrave Macmillan.

Hawkes, T. (1977) *Structuralism and Semiotics.* Berkeley, CA: University of California Press.

Jakobson, R. and Waugh, L.R. (1979) *The Sound Shape of Language.* Bloomington, IN: Indiana University Press.

Jones, J. and Coffey, S. (2013) *Modern Foreign Languages 5–11,* 2nd edn. London: Routledge.

Kramsch, C. (2006) 'From communicative to symbolic competence'. *Modern Language Journal*, 90, 249–52.

Kümmerling-Meibauer, B. (2014) 'What goes on in strangers' minds? How reading children's books affects emotional development'. *Narrative Works: Issues, Investigations and Interventions,* 4 (2), 64–85.

Legg, R. (2009) 'Using music to accelerate language learning: An experimental study'. *Research in Education,* 82 (1), 1–12.

Maun, I. (2006) 'Penetrating the surface: The impact of visual format on readers' affective response to authentic foreign language texts'. *Language Awareness,* 15 (2), 110–27.

McRae, J. (1991) *Literature with a Small 'l'.* Basingstoke, Hants: MacMillan Education Press.

Norton, B. and Vanderheyden, K. (2004) 'Comic book culture and second language learners'. In Norton, B. and Toohey, K. (eds), *Critical Pedagogies and Language Learning.* Cambridge: CUP.

Pickett, G.D. (1986) 'Reading speed and literature teaching'. In Brumfit, C. and Carter, R. (eds), *Literature and Language Teaching.* Oxford: Oxford University Press.

QCA (2004) *National Curriculum: Handbook for secondary teachers in England.* London: Qualifications and Curriculum Authority.

— (2007) *Modern Foreign Languages Programme of Study for Key Stage 3 and Attainment Targets.* London: Qualifications and Curriculum Authority.

Sakari Roiha, A. (2014) 'Teachers' views on differentiation in content and language integrated learning (CLIL): Perceptions, practices and challenges'. *Language and Education,* 28 (1), 1–18.

Sharples, M. (1999) *How We Write: Writing as creative design.* London: Routledge.

Swain, M. and Lapkin, S. (2005) 'The evolving sociopolitical context of immersion education in Canada: Some implications for program development'. *International Journal of Applied Linguistics,* 15 (2), 169–86.

Tannen, D. (1989) *Talking Voices: Repetition, dialogue, and imagery in conversational discourse.* Cambridge: CUP.

Vermeule, B. (2010) *Why Do We Care About Literary Characters?* Baltimore, MD: Johns Hopkins University Press.

Widdowson, H. (1975) *Stylistics and the Teaching of Literature.* London: Longman.

Zunshine, L. (2006) *Why We Read Fiction: Theory of mind and the novel.* Columbus, OH: Ohio State University Press.

Appendix

Table 5.1: Unit of work based on *Le Petit Prince* by Antoine de Saint-Exupéry

> *UNIT OVERVIEW.* In this unit, pupils will understand the storylines of selected chapters of *Le Petit Prince.* They will be able to describe the plot and infer meaning from specific aspects of the story. They will be able to interpret the story to discover more about the cultural dimension of the book and the message of the author.

RESOURCES	AIMS
• Adapted version of some chapters of *Le Petit Prince* • Resources specifically developed to study *Le Petit Prince* • DVD *Le Petit Prince – la planète du temps* (cartoon adaptation).	**All pupils** will be able to describe the main storylines of the chapters studied. They will be able to express their own opinions on their peers' interpretation of the story. They will be able to interpret some specific aspects of the story to go beyond the factual plot of the book. **Some pupils** will be able to describe the plot of the story at length. To do so, they will use a greater range of adjectives and more advanced language such as specific words or expressions they have researched by themselves. They will be able to interpret the story in more depth and express their opinions using a greater variety of vocabulary and constructions.
TEACHING AND LEARNING SEQUENCE • **In bold = understanding and describing skills** • In neutral font = interpreting skills • *In italics = linguistic focus*	**POINTS TO NOTE**
Introduction of the book: • **Understand who the author is and his importance in France.** • **Understand the context of the book.** • **Describe the book cover.** • Infer the storylines according to the book cover.	• Work on listening skills as well as reading skills. • Extract specific and crucial vocabulary from the short presentation to be able to recycle it later on. • Reinforce the present tense of regular verbs if necessary, although this should only be a revision. • Be able to incorporate some vocabulary given to them within a sentence, paying attention to the accuracy of their verbs.

Chapter 1 – What kind of person the narrator is	
• Understand the plot of the chapter.	• Work on pronunciation by reading the chapter out loud as a class.
• Identify the different characters.	• Re-order exercise with pictures to understand the different moments of the chapter.
• Express opinions.	• Work on accuracy of verbs while doing the above activity.
• Express agreement and disagreement.	• Students should then insert a variety of connectives to link the different stages of the story to create a short summary.
• Interpret hidden messages (adults versus children).	
• *Revise adjective agreements of regular adjectives.*	• Work on essential and recurrent vocabulary to access reading comprehension questions in French on the chapter.
• *Introduce the notion of synonyms.*	
• *Learn different question words.*	• Students have to use opinion phrases such as 'à mon avis/ je pense que/je trouve que/ je crois que' to comment on the messages of the chapter. To do so, they are encouraged to compare what adults think and what children think. They should work in groups at this stage.
• *Extend range of connectives.*	
	• Students can use the language of agreement and disagreement to compare their ideas in class discussions. (je suis d'accord/ oui, mais on peut aussi dire/je ne crois pas que etc.)
	• Work on description adjectives to describe adults and children such as 'stupide/marrant/ ignorant/intelligent/malin' etc.

Chapter 2 – The narrator meets 'le Petit Prince' • **Understand the plot of the chapter.** • Express opinions and points of view. • *Carry on working on synonyms and extend the range of synonyms they know.* • *Be able to transpose a passage from the 'je' form to the 'nous' form, working on verb endings.* • *Introduce irregular adjective endings 'eux' and 'if' as well as irregular adjectives.* • *Recycle new vocabulary to comment on a picture.*	• Identify themes in the chapter to support their understanding and justify them by quoting from the text. • Be able to label a few pictures from the original chapter to explain what the picture represents by creating a sentence. More able students will recycle the connectives they have previously learnt. • Work on adjectives endings of irregular adjectives such as 'répétitif/ennuyeux/vieux' etc. and be able to include these in sentences about the chapter.
Chapter 4 – Where Le Petit Prince comes from • **Understand the plot of the chapter.** • **Study pictures from the book and recycle adjectives to describe the pictures.** • Express opinions about the pictures. • Carry on comparing adults with children.	• True or false exercise to understand the storylines. • Extract pictures from Chapter 4 to comment on the appearances of the Turkish astronomer, students use a range of adjectives to describe them and also express opinions by recycling the language they have studied so far. More able students can use more advances phrases. • Use columns to compare what is important for adults and what is important for children when they have a new friend. • Use the above to deduce the message of the author, students use opinion expressions to infer this.

Chapters 11 and 13 – Le Petit Prince meets the businessman and the conceited man • **Understand the plot of the chapter through group work.** • Infer the intonation of the dialogue according to the context and the meaning of the dialogue. • Acting skills. • *Work on pronunciation and reading skills.*	• Students work in groups to complete a worksheet on the chapter they have been allocated, they have to answer comprehension questions to support their understanding of the plot. • Chapter 11 is aimed at weaker ability students and Chapter 13 is aimed at high ability students. Worksheets are designed accordingly. • Students work in groups of three to read out loud and act out the dialogue of the chapter they have worked on. They have to deduce the right intonation according to the meaning of the dialogue. They use the knowledge they already have of *Le Petit Prince* character to represent him as truthfully as possible.
Assessment – Creation of a comic strip of Le Petit Prince book • **Ordering the different events of the chapters studied.** • **Recognizing the different characters.** • **Labelling the pictures according to the story of the book.** • Expressing opinions. • Inferring the ending of the story. • *Using new vocabulary and irregular adjectives within the narrative.* • *Being able to use regular and irregular verbs in the present.* • *Using a range of connectives and sequencing words such as 'd'abord/puis/enfin' etc.*	• Students are given a collection of pictures and a template for their comic strip, they have to re-order the pictures according to the story of the book and write a short caption underneath to create a story. The last picture is left blank for each student to finish the story in the way they wish. They are encouraged to use a range of adjectives, specific vocabulary, connectives and opinion expressions to complete this task.

Looking beyond the book itself	• Students watch an episode of the cartoon adaptation of *Le Petit Prince*. They discuss the similarities and differences compared to the original book and give their opinion using the transferable language they have learnt in the unit as a class discussion.
• Reflecting on a cartoon adaptation of *Le Petit Prince* called *Le Petit Prince – la planète du temps* (on DVD).	

Chapter 6

Breaking out

The use of film in the MFL classroom

Colin Christie and Shirley Lawes

What is distinctive about film as a medium for learning?

Film is an exciting way to enrich learning in the modern foreign languages (MFL) classroom. Its inclusion in schemes of work and lessons might, at first glance, seem precluded by the National Curriculum (NC) (DfE, 2013) as its references to translation, transcription and accuracy may appear to encourage a more traditional approach to the teaching of MFL. The mention of the study of literary texts would seem to reinforce this suggestion and leave little space for the inclusion of film in a school's scheme of work. In an environment increasingly focused on outcomes and the demonstration of student progress, it is easily argued that the incorporation of film into a crowded curriculum is a luxury that cannot be afforded. Closer inspection, however, shows that film can serve a number of the aims listed by the NC. It can, for example, 'foster pupils' curiosity and deepen their understanding of the world', help them 'learn new ways of thinking' (DfE, 2013: 1) and provide content beyond students' 'immediate needs and interests' (ibid.: 2). It also provides a strong motivation to develop comprehension skills and 'express ideas and thoughts' (ibid.: 3).

We might therefore consider the new key stage 3 (KS3) curriculum as looking beyond the immediately transactional and functional uses of language that are presented in directly 'relevant' situations, and reconsider the notion that foreign language learning is a cultural pursuit. Film is an art form and cultural medium that has much potential to enrich the foreign languages (FL) learning experience, in terms of introducing aspects of daily life that give important insights into the countries and people where the foreign language is spoken. It is also an accessible form of 'enrichment culture' (Lawes, 2007: 89) – which includes literature, poetry and art – that is now being emphasized more in the MFL curriculum. How film can enhance the motivation and attainment of learners from an early stage is slowly being recognized as creating 'meanings that matter' for learners (Dearing and King, 2007: 15) through the unravelling of the conventions and layers of meaning that are unique to film as an art form.

In terms of content, film can develop learners' intercultural competence (Pegrum, 2008) and cultural knowledge and give them an unprecedented insight into the target language (TL) culture. This insight is authentic and accessible and places language in context in a unique way. While highlighting the unique aspects of the TL culture, film also serves to reinforce the similarities between students' lives and those of others and help break down potential barriers. Linguistically, film offers an accurate representation of language in use and a 'wealth of contextualised linguistic and paralinguistic terms and expressions' (King, 2010: 510). This means that learners can witness language as a living phenomenon and as a vehicle for communicating meaning in real contexts. Film offers a rich and substantial experience of the 'forms of life' of a culture – with music and voice, performance and setting, all scaffolded by stories that sweep a viewer along. Short films in particular offer very powerful experiences for teachers and learners. They are often more like poems than feature films – rich, densely allusive texts whose stories are told in the language of pure cinema, principally because, as they are mostly only shown in film festivals, it is expensive and counterproductive to use lots of dialogue. Typically, short films, or 'shorts', are only 4–6 minutes in length which means they can be fully explored by students in their entirety. Relevant activities include watching and discussing, inferring and predicting in the TL, and of course learning about a range of film styles, periods and genres. In addition to the linguistic and cultural benefits, film can be a powerful motivator for students who may not always see the immediate relevance of MFL (Ryan, 1998; Lawes, 2011). Indeed, recent classroom-based research has produced convincing evidence of increased motivation among learners using film, and, over time, significant improvements in their confidence and ability to express themselves spontaneously in the TL. Moreover, teaching with film has encouraged teachers to take risks, move out of their routines and comfort zones and rediscover the creativity of teaching (Carpenter *et al.*, 2015).

The software that is now readily available in most schools, to edit and work with clips and film extracts to create teaching resources, makes film a much more accessible medium for use in the classroom. Over recent years there has been a significant amount of curriculum research in developing pedagogical approaches to using film and tracking its impact on learners and teachers. It is now an ideal time to bring film into the FL classroom to regenerate the curriculum content, develop a distinctive cultural focus and above all to encourage learners to see FL learning as an important part of their education.

How film can enrich MFL lessons

A key point to consider regarding film in the MFL classroom is that a film is a work of art, just like a piece of literature, and it must be explored in its own terms for its own worth. It should be seen as *content* rather than simply a *resource* or a vehicle for learning a particular tense or set of vocabulary. The latter can, however, provide a good starting point, setting in train a process of development to realize the full potential of teaching with film. The power of film is in the combination of the image and the word in the construction of a narrative. This is said not to mystify, but to draw attention to the unique potential of film to engage the interest and imagination of learners and to initiate them into this accessible art form. With this in mind, when preparing to use film in the MFL classroom we can then explore its pedagogical potential.

Film can be approached in a variety of ways with a number of differing aims, all of which can be combined. These aims include the development of students' visual literacy (Pegrum, 2008), the improvement of comprehension skills, the reinforcement of language previously learnt, the provision of a stimulus for creative speaking and writing, the enhancing of cultural awareness and the increasing of motivation in general.

Using film as a reinforcement of topic language previously learnt is useful in a context where the teacher feels limited as to the amount of time that can be spent diverging from set topics and language. The description of characters can relate to the topic of personal identity, for example, and a narration of a sequence of events in the film might tie into the topic of daily routine (as in the case study example described later in this chapter). This allows learners to transfer language to another, real context and to practise it in a purposeful way, possibly adding to the vocabulary learnt.

In terms of comprehension skills, learners have the opportunity to listen to dialogue that is situated and contextualized and that can make a welcome change from the disembodied voices of the standard textbook sound file. They can use paralinguistic clues to work out meaning, making the FL more accessible. They are also forced to listen for gist so they may be less fazed at an inability to understand every word.

The benefit of film in terms of the enhancement of cultural awareness is clear, and this can vary according to the film chosen. The cultural input may be historical or geographical, relate to daily life and customs or simply show everyday life through a different lens. The cultural aspect of film has an important role in driving home similarities as well as differences in respect of the TL culture. Pegrum *et al.* (2005: 55) point out how film can 'provide a first taste of the otherness of life instructed in and through the linguistic medium being studied'. However, as Lawes (2000) notes, it is just as important to reinforce the similarities. A focus on such similarities can help lessen the effect of the alienation felt with regard to this culture and increase feelings of empathy and common humanity in learners. Film can throw up universal themes (King, 2010), such as those of love, fear, oppression or celebration and these can be the basis for class discussion and debate, at a simple or more advanced level. Clearly learners will need to be taught the language they need for this, but this is perfectly possible in the TL. Furthermore, interacting with a series of films over time demonstrates to learners that the TL culture is not 'a monolithic entity' (Pegrum, 2008: 146) but rather a rich tapestry of different cultures, just like students' own culture.

Work on the film as text itself (work *on* the text) is but one of three perspectives – the others being work *around* and work *away from* the text. The film can be used as a basis for speaking and writing before viewing, as learners can be encouraged to predict what the film might be about and what might happen in it, drawing on the title, one or more still images from the film, a poster, a short audio sequence, a trailer or short clip. Work away from the text can take the form of creative speaking or writing, for example the creation of a dialogue or diary entry in the voice of a character.

In terms of the development of visual literacy, film can be analysed in the same way that a text is analysed. Its shots, its sequence of scenes and the portrayal of characters can be analysed so that learners 'learn to view' as well as view to learn. Learners of French, for example, can become familiar with French film language – the '*plan américain*' and '*contre-plongée*'. This in itself then becomes a context for learner talk and study which may well be of more interest to learners than the more traditional topics of pets and a description of the bedroom (Lawes, 2011).

In a study of students of English, Seferoğlu (2008) underlines the advantages of using film in the classroom. The study reports how learners found it both enjoyable and rewarding and that it provided benefits in terms of language, non verbal communication and culture. Seferoğlu stresses how purposeful use of film, with clear tasks and active rather than passive engagement, is essential to derive the most benefit from it.

Preparing to teach with film: Experiences with student teachers

The postgraduate certificate in education (PGCE) Secondary Languages course at the UCL Institute of Education provides a meaningful initiation into the use of film in the MFL classroom. The film project takes place in collaboration with the British Film Institute (BFI) and focuses on the development of FL learning materials to be used in conjunction with a short FL film.

Short films are chosen because they can easily be viewed in their entirety if little time is available, leaving space for their exploration within lesson time. Furthermore, they often centre around an easily understandable point or theme, and may have a rather quirky slant on life, appealing to learners. A further advantage identified by student teachers is the fact that short films often contain little or no speech. This means that the focus can be less on comprehension, so the move to productive skills and work 'away from' the film can progress more quickly. As one student teacher put it, 'a short film with not much language is good for getting pupils to produce language and be more creative with it'. Another made the point that work on such films enables the films and ideas to be shared with colleagues teaching different languages due to the non-language-specific nature of the soundtrack.

The project gives student teachers the space to work collaboratively at the end of their PGCE course and share teaching strategies and skills acquired over the length of the course. Such collaborative work is not always possible in busy school departments so this time is particularly valuable to them. Most importantly, the film project is an excellent opportunity for student teachers to use their imagination and creativity in exploring and 'pedagogizing' short films. They draw on all the knowledge and experience gained during the year to produce a sequence of lessons that channels their professional learning through the medium of film.

During the project, student teachers receive input in lecture form from the head of education at the BFI as well as the course tutors and an ICT teaching support analyst on ideas for the exploration of film in the classroom. The teachers form language-specific groups of about four and choose a short film from a list provided, for use with a KS3 class. They are also free to select a film of their choice, but all films are limited to a length of ten minutes as an absolute maximum. Student teachers are then required to map out a broad outline for a sequence of lessons based on all or part of their chosen film. This is the crucial creative stage of the project; it is here that the film is viewed multiple times and ideas discussed about how best to explore its potential. They identify an overall aim and outcome for this sequence of lessons; for example, the students might create a voiceover or subtitles on-screen, perform a role play or a film review in the TL or even plan a short film of their own. Then together, and with some technical support where needed, each group sets about using a software package to 'rip' the film, turning it into lesson material, selecting particular elements for a particular purpose and embedding either visual or sound clips or stills into a presentation software package such as PowerPoint or Prezi. While software offers more creative possibilities for the classroom, its use should not be seen as compulsory. Student teachers are then given a few days to complete the following, ready to present to their peers, in a 15-minute slot per group:

1. An outline for a sequence of lessons.
2. A PowerPoint slideshow of one lesson with film extract(s) embedded in the slides.
3. A worksheet for the class.

The presentation takes place at the BFI whenever possible, or alternatively in a lecture theatre with appropriate projector facilities. The activity types showcased by student teachers in their resources fall into the three categories identified above: before, during and after viewing.

Before viewing

Using a 'Tell me' grid, learners listen to a short extract from the film, without seeing it, and extract information as follows:

Qui? (Character)	*Où? Quand?* (Setting)
Qu'est-ce qui s'est passé? (Story)	Ambience (Mood)

Courtesy of Mark Reid, BFI from Aidan Chambers/ CLPE and Chambers, A. (1993) *Tell Me: Children, reading and talk.* Jackson, MS: Thimble Press.

Figure 6.1: 'Tell me' grid

Ideally, after listening, learners contribute ideas orally to complete this grid (often with prompting from the teacher), sometimes in the TL, using clues from the soundtrack to help them. This can be followed by a viewing of the clip for learners to see if their predictions are confirmed or not. Each quadrant offers both the opportunity for learners to recycle language and to be introduced to new vocabulary and structures, and this activity works at all levels, from beginners to advanced. In terms of technology, the film clip can be embedded into a PowerPoint slide and reduced to a tiny size so that when the film plays it can be heard but not be seen by learners. Further 'before viewing' activities include the following:

- Screenshots of characters from the film are shown and learners are asked to predict their character traits.
- Learners speculate on the title of the film from screenshots, the trailer or still images taken from it. To scaffold this, learners can be provided with a choice of titles.
- As above, learners use images or key words to speculate on the theme of the film, again perhaps choosing from a range of possible options.

Films which are set in a historical or particular cultural context can also have language work attached to them, to familiarize learners with the historical or cultural setting.

During viewing

The theme of prediction and speculation is obviously not limited to activities before viewing of the film, and such activities can also take place in the course of watching. The film can be paused at any point and learners asked to predict what comes next. Once more, this can be from a selection of possibilities in the TL for this to be scaffolded and accessible. Learners can be involved in quick pair-work discussion involving simple language agreement and disagreement, so that they can have a meaningful interaction about interesting content in the target language. Other activities for the 'during viewing' phase are:

- standard listening comprehension activities: gap-fills; reordering events on slips of paper or card; 'wildly waving' a slip of paper or card containing the word or phrase when it is heard;
- translation-based activities, where learners identify a phrase from a selection in English when it is heard in the film in the TL;
- repetition work, perhaps imitating intonation and phrasing of one of the characters, either directly from the screen or with the film paused (Hill, 2002);
- with the sound down, learners can prepare and then speak a commentary of the action taking place, either in the form of a description or of the dialogue taking place.

Regarding the use of subtitles, it is important to balance the danger of students' focusing overly on the subtitles with the demotivating effect of overloading them linguistically (Pegrum *et al.*, 2005). One possible solution is to show subtitles on the first viewing and then use them selectively, depending on the objectives in question.

After viewing

Film clearly provides a rich stimulus for creative work that offers many possibilities for learners and teachers. Learners can be involved in character-based work, creating interviews with or dialogues between characters from the film. They can also write an alternative ending. With short films that are silent, learners can create their own dialogues and record them as a voiceover or as on-screen subtitles. All these activities initiate learners into film as a narrative form and, albeit at a very basic level, they learn to 'read' films and talk about film in the TL. Films that highlight issues of wider interest can also provide material for debates in class, provided that these are carefully scaffolded and that learners have the required language available to them. As Seferoğlu (2008: 8) points out, film can 'provide ... a stimulating framework for classroom discussion'.

In giving their feedback on the project, student teachers expressed how much they enjoyed it, noting its usefulness for their teaching in the coming year and the benefits derived from working collaboratively. As the outcomes of the project are not only presented to the whole PGCE Languages group but also shared with them electronically, student teachers were glad to have this resource for use in their newly qualified teacher (NQT) year and beyond. They also felt they had benefited from the technical input around the use of Windows Moviemaker and the ideas on how to explore film from the tutors and the BFI. One student teacher said she would like to use film on a regular basis as a result of the project, and that the resources would be useful in this regard. The student teachers appreciated that there would be less opportunity for collaborative working in the future and were pleased to have learnt from the ideas, resources and different approaches taken by their peers.

Film in action

The following example provides a good initial model for someone starting out in film with a Year 7 class, and could provide a useful springboard to incrementally deepen the focus on the film content itself. The teacher was working in French with a Year 7 mixed ability class in a co-educational school in Essex. The lesson centred around the short film *Destiny* by Fabien Weibel (2012). This was not a one-off lesson but was integrated into the topic of daily routine, reflexive verbs and the present tense, which the class had been studying. The film shows a man's morning routine being repeated over and over again, with varying bizarre outcomes each time. It has no spoken language, so the emphasis was on language production over comprehension.

To begin with, the teacher displayed the French title of the film, *Le Destin*, and elicited the English from pupils. The starter activity was in the form of a 'Tell me' grid with the four headings in the TL: *Qui?* (Who?); *Où?* (Where); *A quelle heure?* (What time?); *Quoi?* (What?). The teacher checked understanding of the question words then played the first minute or so of the film twice over so that pupils could hear the atmospheric soundtrack but not see the film itself. During this time, pupils had to complete the grid. The activity was effectively differentiated in that the support sheet contained options for learners to circle, for example '*dans une maison*' ('in a house'), '*à huit heures*' ('at 8 o'clock'). The standard sheet had a couple of examples but was otherwise more open-ended. While some learners circled appropriate words on the support sheet, others wrote answers such as '*un personne*' ('one character'), '*la cuisine*' ('the kitchen') and '*le matin*' ('the morning'). Although some language was not totally accurate, learners did well to produce language freely in such a short period of time. The words '*un adult*' ('an adult') and '*une personne*' ('a person') showed an incorrect spelling and gender, and the phrase '*J'habite dans sa chambre*' ('I live in his room') was not transferred correctly to the present context. Nevertheless, such prompt, unsupported production of language for real purposes in authentic contexts was impressive, and can help learners to notice their mistakes when the language has real meaning for them.

The teacher then skilfully asked the class for feedback in the TL. She prompted learners to use '*Je pense que ...*' ('I think that ...') when reporting their predictions to the class, and wrote up this key phrase on the board for reinforcement. While, as stated earlier, it is sometimes argued that work with film is a luxury that cannot be afforded in a crowded scheme of work, inclusion and reinforcement of such phrases with a high transfer value demonstrated effective consolidation of the language of opinions, useful in any context. The teacher also encouraged learners to work out language for themselves and to test hypotheses. One asked how to say 'there is' and made an attempt at (the incorrect) '*il est.*' The teacher provided the correct translation, '*il y a*', and once again wrote this up for reinforcement. This provided an excellent opportunity for learners to encounter and use another high-frequency structure in a genuinely communicative context. Such scaffolding allowed another pupil to produce the complete phrase '*Je pense que il y a une personnage*' ('I think there is one character'). The teacher ignored the minor inaccuracy and maintained the communication by asking '*un enfant, un bébé, un adulte?*' ('a child, a baby, an adult?'), to which the pupil replied '*un adulte*'.

This exchange serves to show that, even at the most basic of levels, learners can interact with real content and cognitive challenge, with a minimum of language. When asked about the setting, one learner started off in English with 'I thought it was ...' but the teacher insisted on French. The learner's response '*Je pense que en ville*' ('I think that in town') was the teacher's opportunity to drill '*c'est en ville*' ('it is in town') with the class, so that the high-frequency structure '*c'est*' ('it is') was made salient. Again, this demonstrated integration of language learning with discussion of real content. The teacher asked '*D'accord ou pas?*' ('agreed or not?'), which prompted another pupil to make the suggestion in French that the action was taking place in a bedroom. The teacher was again able to reinforce with the whole class the '*c'est*' structure.

This sequence continued as the teacher elicited known vocabulary from the class, such as times of day and clock times, and daily routine phrases. The teacher encouraged the class to recycle these known daily routine phrases and interact with her in a speaking exercise to put them in the order in which they appear in the film. Once again, this was differentiated as some learners had the language provided for them to reorder, while others had only new phrases to work with, such as '*il nourrit*' so they could say '*il nourrit le chat*' ('he feeds the cat'). In this part of the lesson, the teacher revisited and reinforced the language learnt in a topic-based context while allowing learners to reuse it in a different context, namely that of talking about a film.

The next section of the lesson shifted from a teacher–pupil focus to a pupil–pupil one. Learners cut out images of the film from a sheet, stuck them onto a storyboard in the order in which they featured in the film and wrote captions underneath to describe the action. They did this enthusiastically, using the support sheet and dictionaries, as necessary, to add phrases such as '*il va en ville*' or '*il va au travail.*' ('he goes to town/work').

Finally, learners added their own ending to the story in the remaining three blank boxes, drawing the action and describing it in French. This was an ambitious but creative activity for the Year 7 class, with limited time in one lesson. With more time available, this aspect might have been developed, but nevertheless pupils did make creditable attempts to provide original endings. Some used known language, resulting in accurate French, such as '*il mange un hot dog*' ('he eats a hot dog'), for example. Others built on known language, but as this was not in pre-learnt chunks it resulted in a degree of inaccuracy: '*il arrive à travailler*' ('he arrives at work'); '*il va au Big*

Ben' ('he goes to Big Ben'). The more ambitious phrases showed a greater degree of inaccuracy as learners tried to create new phrases, perhaps with the use of the dictionary: *'il va sur un ordinateur'* ('he goes on a computer'), *'il est assis descendue'* ('he is sitting down') and *'il est embou-teillage'* ('he is in a traffic jam'). This progression reflects stages of creative construction, as noted by Christie:

> Stage 1: learners use known chunks of language in new contexts and these are largely accurate.
>
> Stage 2: learners use known chunks as the basis for expressing themselves and combine these with their own creative use, resulting in a mixture of accurate and less accurate language.
>
> Stage 3: learners largely abandon known language and are so focused on creating new meaning (often drawing on their first language) that accuracy suffers.
>
> (Christie, 2011: 114–15)

These stages reflect the constant tension in language teaching and learning between fluency and accuracy, or focus on meaning and a focus on form. What is interesting about the Year 7 lesson is that it allowed learners to both recycle known chunks and to expand on these by encouraging the production of new, original meanings. A useful follow-up could be to show learners how to express these new meanings in accurate French. There is a further tension for the teacher: wanting to allow learners to express what they want to say, but also needing to simplify the language so that they are not stretching their language too far beyond what they are able to express. The treatment of error is a key consideration in all language lessons, and work with film should treat error sensitively just as with all models of language.

Hill underlines the need for learners working with film not to be inhibited by the fear of making mistakes, so that the visual material 'is regarded as a friend and not as a stick to beat linguistic competence into learners or as a mirror of learners' painstaking inadequacies' (Hill, 2002: 106). When studying any authentic material, such as music or film, it is imperative that enjoyment and appreciation of the material are not overshadowed by a disproportionate focus on language. As has already been stressed, if the authentic material is used as nothing more than a vehicle for language-focused work, the unique nature of the medium becomes lost – a scenario that must be avoided.

The future for film

Over the years that the PGCE project has been operating, significant numbers of student teachers have been motivated to use film in their lessons, and some have joined a subsequent research and curriculum development project. Recent research and continuing professional development (CPD) programmes with experienced MFL teachers confirm that film can be fully integrated into the MFL curriculum. Teachers very quickly become confident in preparing film for classroom teaching, and the impact on learner motivation, engagement and attainment is immediate and lasting. Film offers the opportunity to step outside the 'topic silo' and, in keeping with NC recommendations, to integrate cultural learning into lessons. In schools where teaching with film has been adopted, teachers have worked collaboratively across MFL departments to adapt schemes of work and prepare films for teaching (Carpenter *et al.*, 2015). Initially this is a time-consuming activity and has required a shift in attitudes and approaches, but the rewards in terms of professional satisfaction and sense of confidence to experiment and take risks are well worth the investment.

Nevertheless, it is important to ensure that the incorporation of film does not become overwhelming for the teacher in the context of an increasingly full curriculum and a growing demand for accountability and measurable outcomes in learning. As one teacher commented, 'you need to fight the fear' of stepping outside the tried and tested, the routine and the formulaic. In the initial stages of working with this approach, integrating film into a scheme of work (rather than as a separate module of study) can make it more manageable and offers the advantage of exposing learners to a variety of styles of film. It also presents film as a natural part of learning a language and its accompanying culture in a way that does not seem forced or artificial. One way of consolidating this understanding would be to include an aspect of the film study, however small, in assessments, as this can help 'ensure that cinema is seen as more than "bolt-on culture"' (Pegrum *et al.*, 2005: 61). While one must take care not to mar the enjoyment of the film by making it into an object of testing, inclusion into an assessment could help give the film greater status and add further credibility to the language-learning process.

Furthermore, a film need not be exploited to the full but may be used with a specific focus in mind and perhaps revisited at a later date. This could be for work on comprehension, on creative and innovative production of language or on cultural input. All these aspects may be addressed in due course, and this need not necessarily be through one or two films but by using a range over time. Clearly, some aspect of comprehension will be needed before focusing on production, but as the examples cited here show, films with no or little language can be ideal for this.

The curriculum content of MFL has, for some time, failed to inspire young people and has needed reinvigorating. As comfortable as transactional language and familiar topics that relate directly to everyday life may be, they represent a limited and limiting view of MFL in the early stages of learning. The new curricula from key stage 2 to A-level could enable teachers to create something new to inspire learners. Cultural learning is an important part of what it means to learn a language, and film is an accessible cultural form that is important in its own right. Learning about film as narrative provides an accessible introduction to other, more challenging, aspects of culture such as literature. Equally, as we have shown throughout this chapter, teaching language through film has much potential to motivate learners and enrich the MFL curriculum. As it becomes a more mainstream activity in languages classrooms, it will help more young people to see MFL learning as an interesting, challenging and engaging area of study.

Acknowledgement
With thanks to Julie Margiotta of The King Edmund School, Rochford, Essex.

Questions for practice

- How could working with short film provide a different focus for learning that helps us move on from 'topic teaching'?
- What new approaches to assessment could be developed?
- How can teaching with film link to other cultural teaching?

Further reading

Practice:
http://londoned.org.uk/general-news/using-film-to-improve-modern-foreign-languages

Theory:
Lawes, S. (2008) 'Reviving the secondary foreign languages curriculum: Film in the French classroom'. *Francophonie*, 38, 24–7.

References
Carpenter, J., Lawes, S. and Reid, M. (2015) 'Screening Languages, British Film Institute'. Online. www.screeninglanguages.org (accessed 13 July 2016).

Christie, C. (2011) 'Speaking spontaneously: An examination of the University of Cumbria approach to the teaching of modern foreign languages'. Unpublished PhD thesis, Institute of Education, University of London.

Dearing, R. and King, L. (2007) *Languages Review*. Online. http://webarchive. nationalarchives.gov.uk/20130401151715/http://www.teachernet.gov.uk/_ doc/11124/LanguageReview.pdf (accessed 13 July 2016).

DfE (2013) *Languages Programmes of Study: Key Stage 3*. Online. www. gov.uk/government/uploads/system/uploads/attachment_data/file/239083/ SECONDARY_national_curriculum_-_Languages.pdf (accessed 1 June 2016).

Hill, B. (2002) 'Video in language learning: Developing oral skills'. In Swarbrick, A. (ed.), *Aspects of Teaching Secondary Modern Foreign Languages*. London: RoutledgeFalmer.

King, J. (2010) 'Using DVD feature films in the EFL classroom'. *Computer Assisted Language Learning*, 15 (5), 509–23.

Lawes, S. (2000) 'The unique contribution of modern foreign languages to the curriculum'. In Field, K. (ed.), *Issues in Modern Foreign Languages Teaching*. Abingdon: Routledge.

— (2007) 'Cultural awareness and visits abroad'. In Pachler, N. and Redondo, A. (eds), *A Practical Guide to Teaching Modern Foreign Languages in the Secondary School*. Abingdon: Routledge.

— (2011) 'Watch and learn'. *The Linguist*, 50 (4), 24–5.

Pegrum, M. (2008) 'Film, culture and identity: Critical intercultural literacies for the language classroom'. *Language and Intercultural Communication*, 8 (2), 136–54.

Pegrum, M., Hartley, L. and Wechtler, V. (2005) 'Contemporary cinema in language learning: From linguistic input to intercultural insight'. *The Language Learning Journal*, 32 (1), 55–62.

Ryan, S. (1998) 'Using films to develop learner motivation'. *The Internet TESL Journal*, IV (11). Online. http://iteslj.org/Articles/Ryan-Films.html (accessed 1 June 2016).

Seferoğlu, G. (2008) 'Using feature films in language classes'. *Educational Studies*, 34 (1), 1–9.

Weibel, F. (2012) *Destiny*. Animated short. Online. www.youtube.com/ watch?v=wEKLEeY_WeQ (accessed 13 September 2016).

Appendix of short films

Non-language-specific:

Tripe and Onions (Martón Szirmai. Hungary, 2006)

Oktapodi (Emud Mokhberi, Julien Bocabeille, Thierry Marchand, Quentin Marmier, François Xavier Chanioux, Olivier Delabarre. France, 2007)

Fresh Guacamole (PES. USA, 2012)

French:

Les Crayons (Didier Barcelo. France, 2004)

Le Bon Numero (Aurelie Charbonnier. France, 2005)

Place des Fêtes from *Paris je t'aime* sequence (Oliver Schmitz. France, 2006)

Quais de Seine from *Paris je t'aime* sequence (Paul Mayeda Berges and Gurinder Chadha. France, 2006)
French Roast (Fabrice O. Joubert. France, 2008)
J'attendrai le suivant (Philippe Orreindy. France, 2002)
Stricteternum (Didier Fontan. France, 2005)
L'Or Bleu (2012)
Bouts en train (Emilie Sengelin. France, 2006)
Madagascar un carnet de voyage (Bastien Dubois. USA, 2011)

Spanish:
7.35 de la Mañana (Nacho Vigalondo. Spain, 2003)
Todo exterior (Mercedes Domínguez. Spain, 2009)
Viaje a marte (Juan Pablo Zaramella. Argentina, 2004)
Abuelo grillo (Denis Chapon. Bolivia, 2009)
Día de los Muertos (Film School Shorts, 2014)
Ana y Manuel (Manuel Calvo. Spain, 2004)
La increíble historia del hombre sin sombra (José Esteban Alenda. Spain, 2008)
Alma (Rodrigo Blaas. Spain, 2009)

German:
Beinahe (Uwe Greiner. Germany, 2010)
Dufte (Ingo Rasper. Germany, 2001)
Schwarzfahrer (Pepe Danquart. Germany, 1993)

Italian:
Notte sento (Daniele Napolitano. Italy, 2008)

Chapter 7

Translation in secondary school languages teaching

Glennis Pye

Translation makes a comeback

When, in 2013, the Department for Education published its new *National Curriculum for England* (NC) and its languages programme of study for key stage 3 (KS3), those concerned with languages teaching in this sector examined it closely to identify what distinguished it from its predecessor, to understand the key areas for development and amend schemes of work accordingly. The following two statements immediately stood out as significant:

> Pupils should be taught to:
>
> • read and show comprehension of original and adapted materials from a range of different sources, understanding the purpose, important ideas and details, and provide an accurate English translation of short, suitable material ...
> • write prose using an increasingly wide range of grammar and vocabulary, write creatively to express their own ideas and opinions, and translate short written text accurately into the foreign language.
>
> (DfE, 2013: 2–3)

Translation had not been a required part of secondary school languages teaching in England at KS3 or 4 since the 1980s when it existed to prepare students for the O-level examinations for languages. When these were replaced by the GCSE in 1986, the obligation to teach translation was removed and, as a result, it disappeared from languages classrooms except in teaching for A-level examinations. Now, translation from, and into, a foreign language was to once again become an aspect of language teaching that teachers in England – obliged by law to follow the new NC from September 2014 – would be required to reinstate in the teaching of foreign languages (FLs) to children aged 11–14.

In 2015, examination boards released their specifications for new languages GCSEs, confirming the expectation that translation from, and into, another language would form part of these examinations too. Translation would be an element of both the reading papers (requiring translation into English) and the writing papers (requiring translation from English) of the languages GCSEs from 2018. Foundation-level candidates would be expected to translate a number of sentences or a short paragraph containing high-frequency language, whereas higher-level candidates would be expected to translate longer texts containing some more complex language.

Secondary school languages teachers have, no doubt, reflected on the changes being required of them (the introduction of translation being just one of these changes), and it can only be expected that opinions and attitudes toward them will vary. Some argue that the changes to the NC and to GCSE examination specifications have come about as a result of the political motivations or personal preferences of policymakers and not as a result of evidence-based research into languages teaching and learning. Those responsible would likely offer the defence that educators have been consulted closely throughout the redesign process. Although here is perhaps not the place for that debate, further research may be needed if the reintroduction of translation is to be fully understood and convincingly justified.

Those involved in languages teaching will have inevitably been language learners and will, to a greater or lesser extent, have carried out translations. How much and what kind of translation they will have done will depend on a range of factors including age and nationality. A languages teacher educated in the UK system during the last 20 years or so is only likely to have experienced translation as part of their A-level course and university degree, whereas an older teacher or, for example, a French teacher educated in France, is also very likely to have carried out translation activities (most likely very traditional in nature) as part of their FL learning from a relatively young age. Experience of, and personal attitudes and beliefs about, the role of translation in language learning will vary accordingly. Some will naturally hold more favourable views than others toward it. Teachers' views on translating as part of their own language learning experience will inevitably inform or colour their views on the place translation should have in languages teaching now. Alongside personal views, however, a professional will also seek out more objective sources of information.

The reintroduction of translation is a significant change and will trigger many questions in the minds of those associated with languages teaching, including the very obvious questions around whether it benefits or hinders language learning and speculation about its absence over such a long period of time. It seems natural to believe or suspect that there were valid reasons for its disappearance from the languages classroom. In the next part of this chapter we will consider these key questions from a more detached and neutral perspective, reviewing first the reasons for the changes in the status of translation in languages teaching over time.

A translation timeline

Let us start by considering the place translation has occupied over the years in languages teaching as a whole, remembering that translation was central to languages teaching and learning at its very beginnings:

> for thousands of years this ancient craft had been right at the heart of language learning. Indeed, of almost all learning, for many of the mediaeval universities developed out of what were originally schools of translation.
>
> (Duff, 1989: 5)

In more recent history, translation was central in what was referred to as the Grammar Translation method that dominated languages teaching for many years. This is clearly demonstrated in this description of the method as:

> a way of studying a language that approaches the language first through detailed analysis of its grammar rules, followed by application of this knowledge to the task of translating sentences and texts into and out of the target language.
>
> (Richards and Rodgers, 2001: 5)

During the late nineteenth and early twentieth centuries, newer methodologies (such as the Direct Method) began to take over. In contrast to the Grammar Translation approach where 'reading and writing are the main focus' and 'little or no systematic attention is paid to speaking or listening' (Richards and Rodgers, 2001: 6), these newer methodologies placed more emphasis on the importance of oral fluency and 'real-life' communication. This was perhaps not surprising, as countries around the world were rapidly becoming much more directly involved with each other. Communicating in other languages was of use to a far greater number of people than ever before. Furthermore, the science of how we learn foreign languages became an area of interest and significant research and, as Cook

(2010: 87) remarks, by the 1970s some of the research into what had come to be known as second language acquisition (SLA) and the resulting theories had begun to have a major impact on languages teaching.

Notably, there was a move, supported by the theories of Stephen Krashen, to remove the use of a learner's first language (L1) from the foreign languages classroom altogether. It was his conviction that a foreign language (L2) could and should be acquired naturally in the way that someone learns their first language, through exposure to 'comprehensible input', and that 'the formal learning of linguistic rules could never impact on real acquisition' (Grenfell and Harris, 2014: 187). In this climate, it is no surprise that the use of translation in language teaching was put to one side since it does, by its very nature, require the use of L1. For secondary school teachers of modern foreign languages (MFL) in England, this shift in attitude and emphasis was reflected in the 1990 NC for MFL, which stated that one of the main aims of teaching a language should be 'to develop the ability to use the language effectively for purposes of practical communication' (DES, 1990). The impulse to banish L1 from the languages classroom at that time was further reinforced by those in the driving seat at the Department of Education and Science (DES), through its famous declaration that 'the natural use of the target language for virtually all communication is a sure sign of a good modern languages course' (DES, 1990).

What perhaps is surprising, as Cook asserts, is that even when, several years later, Krashen's views were challenged by new SLA research and some use of L1 was again deemed to be acceptable, the possible uses of translation in language teaching and how it might be beneficial to learners were not then considered as an area for potential research. Even now there has been no significant research into this area, suggesting that Cook is probably correct when he asserts that 'the notion that translation is not helpful to acquisition seems to have been so firmly established that it has hardly been investigated at all' (Cook, 2010: 88).

Translation, as we have already mentioned, survived in the secondary school languages classroom until the introduction of GCSE examinations in 1986, but since that time has been largely ignored in all sectors. While intermittently referred to it would seem that attitudes toward translation remained largely unchanged. In his book from the late 1980s, Duff points to the fact that translation was still considered as 'not suitable for classroom work because the students must do the writing on their own; it is also time-consuming and wasteful' (Duff, 1989: 5). In this statement we can see that translation was thought of only in terms of the type of activities it entailed as part of the Grammar Translation method – that is to say, written, non-communicative tasks that require individual students to work at length on a piece of text. While the aim of Duff's book, *Translation*, was to revive and rejuvenate the use of translation in languages teaching (in the English language teaching (ELT) sector at least, though it is frequently claimed developments in that sector often serve to inform approaches to secondary school languages teaching), any subsequent change in attitude toward it failed to materialize.

In 2000 the NC stated: 'Pupils should be taught to: Use their knowledge of English or another language when learning the target language' (DfEE, 2000), and this might have been interpreted as a green light for the reintroduction of translation. It seems, however, that negative attitudes toward translation were impossible to shake off. Indeed, we continue to see evidence of this in later attempts to bring translation back to life in the classroom. In another article that aims to reveal 'the hidden potential of translation', Stoitchkov (2006, no pagination) asserts that it continued, all these years later, to suffer from 'too close an association with the Grammar Translation Method'.

Turning our attention to the present, it is now the case that, whatever our attitudes toward the use of translation in languages teaching have been, it is very firmly back on the agenda for the secondary school sector. Significantly, in more recent publications, both the use of L1 and the use of translation have reappeared as areas for discussion in the field of applied linguistics. There are those who feel that the use of L1 has a more important role to play in languages teaching than it has done for a long time. Butzkamm and Caldwell (2009), for instance, call for a much greater use of L1 in the languages classroom, and include the use of translation activities in their vision for this, while Cook (2010) defends the use of translation extensively and emphatically in his book *Translation in Language Teaching*. Much of what Cook has to say in support of translation is proposed through a rigorous and convincing dismantling of the validity of the ideas that have for so long prevented translation from making a comeback, and by clearly describing why it is necessary to reconsider its position.

We must look on the NC requirement to reincorporate translation into our teaching as more than a mere obligation. If we are to engage fully with the use of translation in our practice, we need to reconsider the nature of some of the long-held prejudices against it, and explore the possible forms that translation might take in the secondary school MFL classroom of today. The following section of this chapter describes a series of interventions that were carried out in three London secondary schools. The aim of these interventions was twofold: to establish the extent to which current attitudes toward translation among practising MFL teachers mirror the negative views of the past that have held translation at bay for such a long time; and to examine the types of activity that might appropriately meet the requirements of the NC programme of study and/or be considered effective activities for the teaching and learning of languages. As we have seen, little research into the use of translation in languages teaching exists, either in relation to languages teaching in general or regarding the English secondary school context. These interventions were viewed very much as a starting point for research into this important and long-overlooked area.

Case study

The interventions were carried out within the MFL departments of three state secondary schools in the south west London area (one mixed and two all girls' schools), and were structured as follows:

Part One: Translation workshop and questionnaire

Part Two: Developing and trialling translation materials (in one of the schools)

Part One

During Part One of the intervention, an hour-long workshop was held in each MFL department. Participants were subsequently asked to complete an online questionnaire to reflect further on points that had arisen during the sessions. Each workshop consisted of a general discussion on the subject of attitudes toward translation and its introduction into the KS3 curriculum and GCSE specifications, followed by an exploration of different types of translation activity. The information gathered via these two routes is now examined in relation to the often-stated grounds for opposition to translation in the teaching of languages.

The main argument against the use of translation in languages teaching seems to have been that it encourages learners always to link the foreign language in their minds with their own language and a belief that doing this will hamper progress toward a good level of oral fluency. In the context of a languages teaching climate focused predominantly on communicative methodologies, this was certainly seen as reason enough to banish the use of translation. This argument, however, assumed two things.

The first assumption is that a learner who is not exposed to translation and its inevitable use of L1 will not be as likely to link L1 and L2 as a learner who, on the contrary, is exposed to it. But Cook suggests that, in any case, 'Learners will always relate the new language to their own, even if only in their minds ...' (Cook, 2010: 49). To ignore or even attempt to ban from the languages classroom what would seem to be a natural process in the mind is, surely, at best pointless and, at worst, obstructive. Is it not the case that learners can gain important insights into a range of issues by comparing and contrasting a new language with aspects of their own language, drawing on the knowledge they already have to help develop this new knowledge? As argued by Weschler (1997), it is surely 'better to think of the influence of the L1 on the L2 as a potential aid or tool'. Weschler also offers here a useful description of the role of L1 in the learning of another language when he talks of 'the construction of a glorious new edifice in the mind of the student, wherein the mother tongue acts as the necessary scaffolding to be gradually removed over time.'

The view of the participating MFL teachers regarding this point was that it is indeed the case that learners will always make links in their minds with L1, whether or not they are supposed to, since translation is a 'natural process'. It was stated by one, and others concurred, that links with L1 'come up in one form or another pretty much every lesson', and they expressed the view that it would seem sensible to try to harness this instinctive reaction to support pupils' learning, rather than to ignore it or attempt to supress it. They felt that, although there might be considerable challenges attached to the development of pupils' ability to understand the metalanguage necessary for translation, this could, as well as aiding learners to develop their foreign language skills, also support their literacy skills in general. It could be argued, then, that translation might be used to strengthen pupils' knowledge and understanding of L1 as well as to teach L2.

Where teachers *did* identify an area in need of careful consideration was in the expectations around the use of the target language (TL) in the MFL classroom. When asked to identify the challenges the use of translation activities may involve, many teachers commented on this. One teacher expressed the concern that, 'With the current focus on target language, the teacher will need to think a lot about how translation activities are delivered.' The NC does indeed make clear the expectation that pupils' oral abilities should be thoroughly developed. It states that:

> The national curriculum for languages aims to ensure that all pupils speak with increasing confidence, fluency and spontaneity, finding ways of communicating what they want to say, including through discussion and asking questions, and continually improving the accuracy of their pronunciation and intonation.
>
> (DfE, 2013: 1)

Further references to the need to develop pupils' speaking abilities are present in the NC document and leave us in no doubt that the use of the TL in the MFL classroom will continue to be a focus for teachers. It states that:

> Pupils should be taught to:
>
> - initiate and develop conversations, coping with unfamiliar language and unexpected responses, making use of important social conventions such as formal modes of address;
> - express and develop ideas clearly and with increasing accuracy, both orally and in writing;
> - speak coherently and confidently, with increasingly accurate pronunciation and intonation.
>
> (ibid.: 1–2)

Teachers participating in the workshop agreed that, with careful planning, the use of the TL could be maintained and there could be opportunities for the development of speaking skills during translation activities.

The second assumption in the argument that translation hampers spoken fluency is that translation activities cannot be anything other than academic, written activities in the style of the Grammar Translation method, 'conceived as the polar opposite of "real-world" language and activities, rather than as something interwoven into communication in bilingual contexts' (Cook, 2010: 37). There are a number of observations to be made here. In relation to the design of activities, it is surely possible to create these to address a whole range of aims, including those that develop communication skills, such as speaking and listening skills, for that is what is usually implied when referring to a communicative task. However, any consideration of the meaning of 'communicative' should not fail to also take into consideration the fact that, in the globalized world in which we live, much more of our communication occurs in writing than ever before and this includes our communication via languages other than our own. To be able to translate the written word from, and into, another language is a skill well worth developing for anyone. As Cook (2010: xx) notes, 'an ability to translate is part of everyday bilingual language use – in personal, professional, and public life – and is needed by all learners, not just translation specialists.'

The teachers involved in the workshops were very much in agreement with these views. Translation was seen as a 'valuable skill'; and one teacher's contribution that 'in the world of work, translation is extremely important ... I have always been translating in my jobs – often from languages I haven't formally been taught ...' is representative of the broad consensus.

Another teacher commented: 'it is good that we are moving towards manipulating language on the go rather than just memorizing.' In this she refers to the removal of the GCSE Controlled Assessments to test writing and speaking that many teachers feel are more a test of memory than an ability to write or speak fluently and spontaneously in the foreign language. However, her observation also carries with it the implication that writing can also be considered a communicative activity of high importance. This teacher asserted that being able to translate a previously unseen text is more like the real-life situation in which someone might try to understand (by translation) something seen on the Internet, for example.

The teachers also agreed that translation activities need not be restricted to those of the Grammar Translation method, that they could sometimes be interactive in nature and that there exists, in the use of translation, enormous potential to develop activities to support a whole range of skills vital for effective language learning. During the workshops, a range of translation activities were explored with this in mind. These included, for example, activities that support the teaching of:

- vocabulary
- grammatical structures
- listening skills
- speaking skills
- cultural knowledge and understanding.

Teachers voiced very positive attitudes toward the different activity types, agreeing that they could be motivating and engaging for pupils. In particular, it was unanimously accepted that translation need not and should not be restricted to the traditional written tasks of the past, which lacked variety and were, for many, a daunting prospect. Translation, it was agreed, could be conceived and delivered to a broad range of pupils in many different forms, including through tasks of a more active nature. Notably, these teachers also believed that translation aids a learner's understanding of the concept that two languages do not always map onto each other directly and that a word-for-word approach to expressing oneself in another language is not always successful. Cook (2010) also suggests that learners who do not carry out translation as part of their language learning are much more likely to make the mistake of using what he refers to as 'word-for-wordism' than those who do.

Most teachers of MFL will be familiar with the sometimes amusing but often frustrating appearance of literal translations from English into L2 in pupils' work – such as 'It [the football match] was a tie', translated as '*C'était une cravate*', for example – or with pupils' bemusement at the literal English translation for a term in L2. For example, a pupil may ask 'Why is the word for girlfriend '*une petite amie*' when she might not be small at all?' Indeed, reaching an understanding that language can be used both literally and idiomatically is an important step in becoming an effective language learner since only once the dangers of 'word-for-wordism' have been realized can steps be taken to avoid them.

The idea that translation might take the form of communicative activities was strongly supported. For example, the following activity, with a focus on listening skills, was felt to have potential as a successful activity type:

Step 1 Pupils listen to a song in the language they are learning and are given strips of paper on which some key vocabulary from the song is written in English.

Step 2 The pupils hold up the correct English word whenever they hear it in the song.

Step 3 The pupils work in pairs to translate the words back into the new language, paying particular attention to phonetic rules as a guide to spelling.

Following the workshop, several of the teachers reported having trialled this activity with their classes and that they found it to be effective in several ways. They found that pupils enjoyed the active nature of the tasks and engaged fully in the process of translation it required of them. Furthermore, since the words occurred often in the song, the repeated exposure to them aided pupils' ability to memorize them, and their ability to pronounce the words correctly as well as write them correctly was improved simultaneously. This supports the idea that translation can help develop a range of skills in the learner. Finally, teachers commented on the ease with which they were able to assess each pupil's ability to carry out the activity.

Similarly positive accounts were shared about a translation activity with a focus on speaking and listening skills. This activity requires pupils to work in pairs and, in the following example, requires translation from and into Spanish.

Step 1 Pupil A is given a text in Spanish while pupil B is given an incomplete English translation of this text. For example:

Pupil A: *Pasa mucho tiempo en Internet – ¡al menos tres horas al día! Su madre dice que debería hacer más ejercicio.*

Pupil B: He spends _____ on the Internet – at least _____! His _____ says he should _____.

Step 2 Pupil A reads the text to pupil B, who has to complete the translation, using the TL to ask Pupil A, for example, to repeat or spell a word, to slow down, etc.

Step 3 Without looking at the original, both pupils work together to translate the now-complete English text back into Spanish.

Teachers were of the opinion that pupils would enjoy the challenge that this and other translation activities offer, since their very tangible outcomes can be highly motivating.

Part Two

During the workshops, some observed that, beyond the benefits to language learning that translation can offer, there is also enormous potential for translation to support the development of the learners' cultural knowledge. This notion formed part of the third stage of the intervention when a set of materials was developed and trialled in the form of a translation master class with a group of Year 8 pupils. The intention of the master class was to introduce pupils to the concept of translation, to begin to develop some initial translation skills and to foster positive attitudes toward it. The materials were developed around the topic of holidays for French, already and very recently studied by the pupils, and included:

- PowerPoint – an introduction to translation;
- a set of vocabulary cards in French (including ten key words from the song *C'est les vacances* by Ilona Mitrecey);
- an English version of vocabulary cards plus five extra cards with other words not featured in the song;
- a worksheet – a grid with one column listing the ten English translations of the words in the song and one blank column;
- a set of eight signs showing short exclamations in French celebrating the holiday season (*Enfin les vacances!*, *Youpi! C'est les vacances!*, *Vive les grandes vacances!* and so on);
- a postcard written in French.

The master class incorporated a range of translation activities and consisted of three stages:

Stage 1: Teacher-led introduction to key translation skills and class discussion.

Stage 2:

1. Pupils looked at the English vocabulary cards to: predict which ten of these words they would be likely to hear in a song about holidays; predict which words they would not be likely to hear; and arrange the cards into two columns accordingly. Pupils also discussed in pairs what the French translations for these words were.
2. *C'est les vacances* was played, and pupils listened out for the French translations of the English word cards they had predicted would be in the song. While listening, they were prompted to rearrange any cards they had previously placed in the wrong column.
3. Using the worksheet, pupils translated as many of the words as possible, drawing on what they had heard in the song and comparing spellings with their partner. They then verified their translations by using the set of French word cards.

Stage 3:

1. Pupils worked in groups (taking the role of a translation agency with a mission to complete, in competition with the other agencies) to come up with the best possible English translation for each of the signs.
2. Pupils were shown the postcard but not the message that had been written on it in French and that incorporated many words and phrases from the earlier activities. They read an English version of the postcard and, working in pairs, translated it into French. Their challenge was to try to produce a translation as near to the postcard text as possible.

Pupils responded extremely positively to all of the translation master class activities, and both pupil and teacher feedback on the session showed that carefully designed translation activities could be beneficial in many ways. Many of the pupils found translating 'fun' and 'interesting'. One pupil commented that translating one of the signs ('*L'école est finie – vive les grandes vacances!*') 'was hard, but it was quite fun because it didn't have to be literal.' The teacher also noted how much the pupils enjoyed thinking about how to make their English translations sound as natural as possible and how they worked hard to avoid using word-for-word translations. For example, one group proposed 'School's out!' as a translation of *'L'école est finie'*, and another group held an interesting discussion on whether to translate *'Youpi!'* as 'Yay!' or 'Yippee!'. Once made aware of the importance of thinking beyond the literal, pupils enjoyed the freedom and challenge of coming up with the most natural-sounding English, and demonstrated admirably their ability to move away from 'word-for-wordism' to achieve this.

All agreed, unsurprisingly, that translating into French was more difficult, but this did not seem to dishearten them. One pupil commented: 'I found English to French harder but I enjoyed testing my skills', providing us with a sense that the challenge offered by translation is, indeed, one that learners can enjoy.

The pupils' cultural knowledge was developed through the use of the song (a very typical French pop song aimed at young teenagers and quite different in style from the type of pop music they were used to hearing) and through some of the signs used. Pupils learned, for example, through considering how best to translate the term *'les grandes vacances'*, that the French school summer holiday is much longer than the English one. It is also worth noting that the development of cultural knowledge is a key feature of the new NC.

Translation: A welcome returner

In conclusion, based on the evidence emerging from these initial investigations into the use of translation in the teaching of languages, it seems likely that the objections toward it that existed in the past no longer seem valid, at least in the context of the English secondary school. Indeed, many teachers have been informally using translation activities in their practice for some time and are enthusiastic about its reintroduction into the curriculum and examination specifications. Of course, there is now an obligation to incorporate translation, but while this may have been the catalyst for its re-emergence, there is every hope that it will be embraced and developed in new and exciting ways that will only serve to support pupil progress in many aspects of language learning.

Questions for future practice

As part of the workshop discussions, the following two aspects of translation use were raised as areas of possible concern, in need of further consideration:

- How should translation be assessed? To what extent should correct spelling and grammatical accuracy be required for marks to be awarded? Some teachers had had experience of a marking approach in which marks were deducted from a score as errors were identified, often resulting in low marks and negative attitudes toward translation on the part of pupils. Are there other more positive and productive ways of assessing translation?
- Will translation put English as an additional language (EAL) pupils at an unfair disadvantage? This was an area of major concern for many of the teachers. They felt that EAL pupils often perform better in languages than in other subjects since their lower level of English does not hinder their progress in the way it does in other subjects. In addition to this, their ability to operate via a language other than their own first language is already more developed than that of other pupils. Some felt that translation could support EAL pupils in their use of English, affording them the opportunity to practise using English at a lower level than in other subjects. What do you think? Do the disadvantages of translation outweigh the advantages for EAL pupils, and, if so, are there ways to manage this?

Further reading

Hawkes, R. (2014) *Teaching Translation in Key Stage 3 MFL*. Online. www.youtube.com/watch?v=i5sHXsUYAZY (accessed 1 June 2016).

Smith, S. (2015) 'An Approach to Translation Which Keeps the Emphasis on Target Language'. Online. http://frenchteachernet.blogspot.co.uk/2015/07/an-approach-to-translation-which-keeps.html (accessed 1 June 2016).

— (2015) *Twenty Ways of Doing Translation into English*: Online. http://frenchteachernet.blogspot.co.uk/2015/03/20-ways-of-doing-translation-into_25.html (accessed 1 June 2016).

References

Butzkamm, W. and Caldwell, J.A.W. (2009) *The Bilingual Reform: A paradigm shift in foreign language teaching*. Tüblingen: Gunter Narr Verlag.

Cook, G. (2010) *Translation in Language Teaching*. Oxford: Oxford University Press.

DfE (2013) *National Curriculum in England: Languages programmes of study: Key Stage 3*. Online. http://tinyurl.com/j2op8ot (accessed 1 July 2016).

Duff, A. (1989) *Translation*. Oxford: Oxford University Press.

Grenfell, M. and Harris, V. (2014) 'Learning strategies, autonomy and self-regulated learning'. In Driscoll, P., Macaro, M. and Swarbrick, S. (eds), *Debates in Modern Languages Education*. Oxford: Routledge.

Richards, J. and Rodgers, T. (2001) *Approaches and Methods in Language Teaching*. Cambridge: CUP.

Stoitchkov, R. (2006) *How to Use Translation in the Language Classroom*. Online. www.beta-iatefl.org/1202/blog-publications (accessed 15 June 2015).

Weschler, R. (1997) 'Uses of Japanese (L1) in the English classroom: Introducing the functional-translation method'. *The Internet TESL Journal*, III (11). Online. http://iteslj.org/Articles/Weschler-UsingL1 (accessed 1 June 2016).

Formative assessment as context for developing autonomous language use and language learning

Marian Carty and Judith Rifeser

Setting the scene

With the return of end-of-course testing in the new GCSE in 2016, the teachers in Orleans Park Modern Languages department wanted to ensure that all the work and effort expended on developing highly successful formative assessment approaches and creative and engaging controlled GCSE assessment tasks would not be lost.

This project was initially launched as part of the newly qualified teacher (NQT) research project by Judith Rifeser in close collaboration with the MFL department. It aimed to investigate assessment for learning strategies and devise assessment tools that would raise learners' grammatical awareness and understanding of the GCSE grade criteria, to improve their overall accuracy. At the same time, these tools needed to be pupil-friendly to facilitate students' self- and peer-correction and enable them to explore the language in their own terms through assessment for learning, thus giving them ownership over their learning. These assessment tools would be used by both pupils and teachers to identify strengths and areas for development.

For over ten years, the department had been using an interactive approach, which places the target language (TL) at the centre of learning as the 'natural means of communication in the classroom' (Christie, 2013: 1). Grammar was first taught implicitly and then explicitly through the TL. However, when it came to feedback on written work, English was used. The department saw this as a missed opportunity; they felt that formative assessment, just like grammar, could provide a meaningful context for pupils to interact 'with and through the target language, receiving and expressing meanings that are important to them' (Little, 1991: 42). They found that using the TL to reflect on their progress, through peer- and self-assessment strategies, developed their pupils' autonomy as both language users and as language learners. Through raising their grammatical awareness, their accuracy in both writing and speaking has improved considerably.

We would hope that this project could serve as an opportunity for departments within, and across, PGCE partnerships to review, revise and innovate. By collaborating, we, as teachers and PGCE training facilitators, can begin a new process of creating locally devised assessments without the imposition of national levels, which may allow us to take into account our particular school context, pupils' learning needs and personal interests. This approach will also support us in engaging with content that helps pupils develop as citizens of the world as well as language learners. Teachers and learners can share in a process of assessment that promotes deep-seated learning and includes a diversity of integrated skill task types that takes into account the 'messy business' that is learning.

The national picture

The challenges facing teachers and teacher-educators of MFL are considerable. We are dealing with a new National Curriculum (NC) for key stage 2 (KS2) and KS3, new GCSE and A-level examination specifications and the promotion of school-based teacher training via School Direct, favoured by the current administration over university-based PGCE programmes. All these changes are occurring against a backdrop of reduced funding and increasing teacher and university lecturer workloads, leading to local and national fragmentation of our education system as the government's 'academization' agenda is pursued, resulting in the virtual disappearance of local education authorities (LEAs).

Previously, LEAs, working with universities, were at the forefront of progressive education supporting the grassroots Graded Objectives in Modern Languages (GOML) movement which assured the place of languages as a subject in a broad and balanced curriculum (Pachler *et al.*, 2005). Many LEAs were strong advocates of Languages for All and saw the highly successful introduction of MFLs into a range of special schools.

The new National Curriculum

So what's new at KS3? Here is a list that Goldsmiths' subject mentors outlined as new or as having greater emphasis:

- speaking with fluency and accuracy;
- translating from the TL into English;
- translating from English into the TL;

- reading and responding in the TL to literary texts;
- dictating or transcribing;
- writing creatively and accurately.

At first glance this could seem like a return to the Grammar Translation method, but such a course of action would not meet the requirements to speak with fluency and accuracy or write creatively. Instead we could see the changes as an opportunity to review and reassess the current orthodoxy and we can surely welcome the removal of NC levels from the assessment arena. The fixation on climbing the level ladder and describing progress in numbers does not 'do justice to the breadth, complexity and sheer messiness of learning' (Yandell, 2013: 17). The almost lesson-by-lesson reference to NC levels to provide data showing progress, which has taken place in many languages classrooms, has not helped to halt the decline in numbers taking a GCSE in languages.

In some of the London schools in our Goldsmiths PGCE partnership, over 90 per cent of pupils opt to study a language at KS4, but the picture in some schools is very worrying indeed, with languages in danger of becoming a minority subject. Ofsted (2011) reports on a decline in competence in speaking, poor reading skills, limited writing, over-reliance on textbooks, over-emphasis on nouns and little awareness of grammar, with the result that learners are unable to generate language to express what they want to say. In those schools where the overwhelming majority of pupils opt to continue studying a language in KS4, they do so because they enjoy languages and feel they are successful. They can communicate what they want to say, have sufficient grammatical awareness to generate language to express original thoughts and have developed a curiosity about the TL and the communities and countries where it is spoken.

Clearly, teachers and schools need to collect information regarding learners' progress and share that information with learners and their carers. However, reliance on tests, more often than not end-of-module tests in listening, reading and writing, is reductive and can often be stress-inducing. Summative tests (including GCSE) assess a very small sample of language. Success is often dependent on luck, and the resulting information does not give a full picture of what a pupil knows and is capable of doing in the language. We seem to have entered the world of 'the emperor's new clothes' by recording progress using NC levels, which describe proficiency in terms of an increasing accuracy of performance, whereas 'research into language development has clearly shown that L2 learning is a much more complex and recursive process with multiple interconnections and backslidings, and complex trade-offs between advances in accuracy, fluency and complexity' (Mitchell, 2003: 17).

In other words, the representation of linguistic progression as exemplified in the former NC levels, has not drawn on current research that concerns inter-language development in secondary classrooms (ibid.). Kohn (2011) contends that 'a "grading orientation" and a "learning orientation" have been shown to be inversely related' (Kohn, 2011: 1). A grading emphasis has a detrimental impact on intrinsic motivation and tends to impact negatively on the quality of a learner's thinking, in that they learn what they need for the test without thinking critically or gaining a deep and useful understanding of the subject they are studying (Mitchell, 2011). Therefore, it could be argued that the removal of NC levels is a step forward toward developing a more holistic, realistic and credible approach to assessing progress.

Since the introduction of GSCEs in 1988, the format has remained largely the same, with only minor modifications up until 2010. The introduction of controlled assessments, allowing teachers the option of devising and customizing assessment tasks to meet the learning needs and personal interests of their learners more meaningfully, was a step in the right direction in terms of reclaiming our autonomy as education professionals. The fact that 60 per cent of the marks could be awarded to locally controlled teacher-devised assessment tasks was recognition of teachers' expertise and responsibility, and conveyed trust and respect toward colleagues in schools. These teacher-devised controlled assessments also enabled teachers to make space for pupil voice, through consultation on content, broadening error-correction techniques to support learning and autonomy and making them participants in the assessment process. For example, in preparation for one controlled assessment on the topic of homelessness, the task instruction was for students to adopt the persona of a homeless person, based on a previous scheme of work that linked directly to the GCSE specification but focused on the stories of real homeless people and their lives and aspirations. Students were made aware of the circumstances that can lead to homelessness and thereby developed their capacity to empathize and challenge stereotypical ideas while further developing their linguistic proficiency. This stands in contrast to exam board-set topic titles whereby students can be rote-learning semi-understood passages for regurgitation in the exams.

The latest reforms are essentially regressive and a return to the pre-2010 approach, plus a smattering of pre-1988 GCE O-level, with the inclusion of translation into English in the reading paper, translation from English into the TL in the writing paper and a response in the TL to a literary text. That we are still assessing our learners 'in an outmoded four skills' pattern, which predates the communicative era' (Mitchell, 2003: 17), is lamentable, but unsurprising given the fixation on the 'golden age' of the GCE O-level of current and recent politicians overseeing education. The assessment of discrete skills has no basis in learning theory and is in contradiction with the idea that there is a symbiotic relationship between L2 input and L2 output. The return to centrally controlled, standardized end-of-course assessment will not take into account the complexity of learning a language. Instead, it will be cruder, more simplistic and with little or no validity – an unreliable indicator of learners' proficiency.

We now turn our attention to assessment for learning strategies, approaches and task types at KS3, in the earlier years of study of the MFL. 'Assessment for Learning is any assessment for which the first priority in its design and practice is to promote pupils' learning' (Wiliam, 2009: 8). Wiliam describes the primary purpose of assessment for learning (AfL) as that of providing feedback to both learner and teacher, which will inform future planning of teaching and learning tasks. Furthermore, he emphasizes that the aim for AfL is *not* to 'serve the purposes of accountability, or of ranking, or of certifying competence' (ibid.: 8).

Exploration of approaches

To understand the process of how formative assessment can be used to support students in developing autonomous language learning and language use, it will help to understand some of the key concepts that lie at the heart of the approaches and methods used in the context-embedded teaching at Orleans Park and the PGCE MFL programme at Goldsmiths.

A fundamental reference point is Swain's (1985) idea of the importance of comprehensible output, which questions the earlier idea by Krashen and Terrell (1983) of the sole emphasis on comprehensible input. Doughty and Williams (1998: 238–9) make use of Swain's discussion on pushed output to argue that both input and output are important for the learner. In other words, as mentioned in the previous part of this chapter, it is crucial to recognize the interdependent relationship between L2 input and L2 output which, in turn, necessitates a consideration of the interplay of the four language-learning skills. In practical terms, this means recognizing the interrelated nature of the four skills and therefore the necessity to devise integrated-skill learning tasks.

By doing so, it is possible, according to Long (1988, 1991) to achieve what he called 'focus on form', an approach that stands in contrast to 'focus on formS' as summarized in Doughty and Williams (1998: 3–4). The key word in the latter approach is 'isolation', thus an isolated treatment of grammar, while the former 'consists of an occasional shift of attention to linguistic code features – by the teacher and/or ... students – triggered by perceived problems with comprehension or production' (Long and Robinson, 1998, cited in Doughty and Williams, 1998: 3). The emphasis should be on how to '*integrate* attention to form' (Doughty and Williams, 1998: 261) in the learning process, and the essential precondition of 'focus-on-form instruction is that meaning and use must already be evident to the learner' (ibid.: 1998: 4).

These ideas underpin our approach to teaching and learning, and support Doughty and Williams's central notion that attention is drawn to grammar only once the students are confident with the language, understand the meaning and are able to use it in context. As a result, with this idea in mind, grammar is not taught as a separate, stand-alone unit. Rather, it becomes part of the lesson that can take the form of guiding the students toward a grammatical point, or the grammatical element discussed might arise from a student's question or error in comprehension or production of the L2. Most important in the use of this approach, however, is the fact that students must be familiar and confident with both the language used to exemplify a grammatical point *and* the language and structures that provide the stimulus for talking about grammar itself.

Focus on form does not only occur as a result of the issues that 'arise incidentally in lessons' (Long, 1991, cited in Doughty and Williams, 1998: 4), but is very often clearly planned into the lesson. This demands students' engagement in their own learning through 'noticing', 'hypothesis formulation and testing' and 'metatalk', the latter referring to an awareness of the learner's own language to think about the use of language (Swain, 1998 in Doughty and Williams, 1998: 238–9).

These key notions provide the preconditions for achieving spontaneous pupil talk – moments that give the learner 'something to say' (Harris *et al.*, 2001: 2). Only then can we prepare the ground for students to develop automaticity, over time, in a positive and encouraging environment, and move away from Krashen and Terrell's (1983: 20) idea that places comprehension before production. Instead, the establishment of routines and the possibility to retreat to the L1 if necessary (Harris *et al.*, 2001) provide a safe and stress-free environment for learning.

Language learning behaviour in GCSE lessons demonstrates the process of developing explicit knowledge (ibid.: 112–14) to adapt to new situations and standardized assessments. This process takes us from Chomsky's earlier distinction between 'competence' and 'performance'

(Chomsky, 1957 and 1965, cited in Johnson, 2001: 51) to a division of the two types of knowledge into 'knowledge about' and 'knowledge how to', respectively (Johnson, 2001). Johnson highlights the importance of both procedural knowledge for spontaneous talk and declarative knowledge. The latter offers the advantage of high 'generativity' (ibid.: 83) and is easily applicable to new situations, demanding relatively little thinking capacity once the rule is learned. By providing knowledge on grammar, embedded in the process of language learning within a context, students will eventually acquire a grammatical understanding that they can fall back on when the need arises. However, Mitchell (1994), in reference to communicative language teaching (CLT), notes that not enough focus has been placed on form in language learning lessons, which, in turn, has led to students not acquiring enough declarative knowledge during the language learning process.

Another aspect to consider, as Lawes (2000) highlights, is the importance of positive emotions connected with successfully being able to communicate, to build confidence and therefore further aid learning. Feedback is essential in this context as it provides learners with knowledge of how successful their performance has been (Widdowson, 1990: 90), enabling them to gradually move to the productive 'generation of new utterances' (Myles, 1998: 323). The *Common European Framework* (2001) provides a useful basis for feedback, as a reference guide that is 'comprehensive, transparent and coherent', providing 'objectives which are at once worthwhile in terms of learner needs and realistic in terms of their characteristics and resources' (Council for Cultural Co-operation, 2001: xii). The document was created as a framework to support teachers and learners alike, focusing on descriptors that aim to build the learners' knowledge of the language they are learning, as well as their independence and confidence (ibid.: xii), instead of restricting them to a certain level for assessment and feedback. With levels being scrapped in the NC in MFL, this framework provided a useful starting point during the course of this project as we sought to extend what we had learned from the initial research and develop AfL tools in the TL across the key stages.

Setting up the project

These issues surrounding AfL became part of the project we are presenting here. The aim of the project was twofold: to devise assessment and feedback tools in the target language, and to implement implicit and explicit grammar teaching in our context-embedded approach.

Our goal was to raise the learners' grammatical awareness and accuracy in the TL by giving them the confidence to take ownership of their learning, to self-correct and develop a deeper insight into how language works (see Harris *et al.*, 2001). We devised simple TL phrases and prompts to help learners develop strategies to not only become more accurate in the TL but to also develop the skills to self-correct and talk about grammar in the TL.

Context-embedded assessment for learning for GCSE controlled-writing tasks

Orleans Park is an average-sized school that recently also opened a sixth form:

> The school has considerably more boys than girls. The number of students known to be eligible for free school meals is below the national average. Around 70% of students are from a White British background and the proportion of students from minority ethnic groups is above the national average, as is the percentage of students who speak English as an additional language. The proportion of students with special educational needs and/ or disabilities is just above the national average; however the percentage with a statement of special educational needs is more than twice the national average.
>
> (Ofsted Inspection report, 2011, Orleans Park)

The languages department comprises specialists in French, German and Spanish and all learners are taught in mixed-ability classes. All language lessons are taught in the target language, including the teaching of grammar, an approach outlined in Harris *et al.* (2001) and exemplified in Christie's work (2013). Both the take-up of languages at KS4 (over 90 per cent) and GCSE examinations results have improved considerably since adopting this interactive, communicative approach. The department works closely with its university PGCE tutors to develop practice, hosting subject mentor meetings and contributing to the PGCE course via 'guru visits', whereby beginner teachers observe live lessons and participate in feedback with the serving teachers.

The initial NQT project was undertaken over a three-month period in KS4 German and focused on preparation for the first controlled assessment of a mixed-ability class. This project was launched as a result of the need identified by the department to raise grammatical awareness and accuracy of our learners at KS4. In accordance with the aims of the NC (2013), we designed lessons to develop pupils' competences, skills and accuracy in grammatical rules, applying them to new situations in KS4. In addition we aimed to provide feedback that was both consistent and in the TL, to allow pupils to talk about their progress and become more independent learners (Council for Cultural Co-operation, 2001).

These are some of the questions the department posed when designing the lessons:

- How can we involve our learners in reflection and review to make them more confident and independent in noticing their mistakes and errors?
- How can we make our assessment and feedback most useful in terms of language learning and most efficient in terms of teacher time expended?
- How can we ensure that the criteria for success are made explicit and integrated into the teaching and learning?
- How can we ensure that the tools created take into account the process as well as the outcome?

In addition, as part of a school-wide initiative to improve feedback and learning, pupils were asked to give their opinion about what they found to be most important when receiving feedback. Overall, the pupils' responses could be summarized into three major points. First, they wanted to know how to improve and be taught how to make these improvements. Second, they felt they needed to be given more time to make improvements. Prompt feedback from the teacher would allow more time for them to re-draft and correct their work. Third, they wanted to know how their work linked to their attainment. In response to the needs of our learners, this project had to address the following key questions:

- How can we make AfL focused and useful as well as time efficient?
- How can we assist learners in becoming independent and confident about correcting their own mistakes?
- How does our feedback translate into GCSE grades?

A successful outcome of the project would translate into pupils' being able to demonstrate grammatical awareness and a high degree of accuracy in German. In addition, they would need to understand the feedback criteria and the link to the GCSE criteria in the TL, as well as be able to talk about grammar in the TL. They also needed to be aware of their current attainment and to have acquired strategies and tools to know how to improve. Finally, feedback needed to be constructive and conducted in the TL (with pupils being able to talk about their own progress), consistent across the department and transferable to the other key stages. Lesson planning had to be adapted on a day-to-day basis, therefore, salient features of grammar had to be highlighted within the everyday classroom context.

Figure 8.1 shows an example of a display created to remind pupils of key grammatical rules in the TL and to reinforce the use of these grammar rules. Common errors and misconceptions that had arisen from previous writing tasks were displayed, for example '*Ich habe keine hausaufgaben*' ('I have no homework'). Pupils then discussed in pairs what was wrong with this sentence. They used Figure 8.1 to reinforce their argument, stating the rule in the TL. A possible answer from a pupil could be: '*Ich denke, "hausaufgaben" ist falsch. Alle Nomen schreibt man groß.*' ('I think "homework" is wrong. All nouns are capitalized'). This is an essential rule in the German language. Nonetheless, the language to voice the explanation is simple.

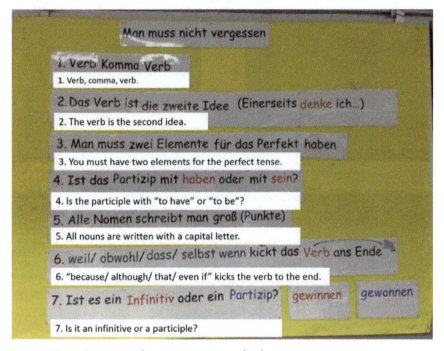

Figure 8.1: Target language grammar display

Figure 8.2 shows a translation activity that was first done individually, then peer-assessed and, lastly, self-corrected. It focuses on word order specific to the German language: '*Das Verb ist die zweite Idee.*' ('the verb is the second idea'). All the necessary vocabulary was taught prior to this activity. These sentences had been written by different learners in their previous homework, and pupils had continuously made this specific mistake. We used their writing to give this translation task meaning and personal significance.

Translation is a regular feature in our lessons not only as a semantic tool but also as a focus on form.

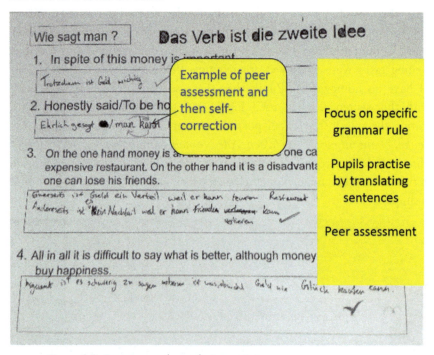

Figure 8.2: Peer-assessed translation activity

The self-assessment sheet (*Selbstevaluationsblatt*), as shown in Figure 8.3 (see Figure 8.7 for translation), was used to periodically assess the learners' progress. It is divided into three parts:

- Part 1, '*Man muss (darf) nicht vergessen*' ('One must not forget'), shows a list of grammar rules that pupils are familiar with and must refer to when checking their own work or peer-assessing.
- Part 2 is a personal comment for the student, written in the TL, using words they are confident with, to identify what they are doing well and highlight areas for improvement.
- Part 3 is a pupil-friendly translation into the TL of the GCSE grade criteria for content, language and grammatical accuracy and spelling. The grid allows for pupils to see what their current grade is but also gives clear guidance on how to improve to achieve a higher grade.

The pupils are given time to make improvements before returning their work for second marking and they are able to see in which areas they are already working at a higher grade.

Man muss nicht vergessen:

1. Wenn diese Konnektive zu Beginn sind (selbst wenn , obwohl , wenn , als , bevor,), muss man Verb – Komma - Verb benutzen.
2. Das Verb ist hier die zweite Idee (Einerseits <u>denke</u> ich / Zum Schluss <u>ist er</u>).
3. Man muss TMP (Time / Manner /Place) richtig haben (Gestern bin ich mit dem Auto nach Deutschland gefahren).
4. Man muss die Endungen der Verben richtig haben (ich denke, du denkst, er/sie denkt, wir denken , ihr denkt , Sie/sie denken) .
5. Man muss zwei Elemente für das Perfekt haben. Ich habe gestern gewonnen.
6. Ist das Partizip mit haben oder mit sein? (ich bin gegangen, er hat verloren).
7. Diese Konnektive kicken das Verb weil / obwohl / dass / wenn /damit / bevor (...weil wir verloren haben/ ich denke, dass er gewinnen wird).
8. In der Zukunft und im Konditional ist der Infinitiv am Ende (Er wird das Spiel <u>gewinnen</u>, ich würde nach Hause <u>gehen</u>).
9. Alle Nomen schreibt man groß (Schule, Noten).
10. Man muss den Komparativ richtig benutzen (besser als../ freundlicher als...).
11. Man muss den Superlativ richtig benutzen (am lustigsten).
12. Ist es ein Infinitiv oder ein Partizip? gehen gegangen.
13. Man muss Wörter nicht vergessen Ich bin nach Deutschland gefahren.
14. Diese Konnektive (und , aber , denn) können das Verb **nicht** kicken. Sie haben keine Effekte.
15. Das Partizip ist am Ende (Ich habe gestern gewonnen).
16. Man muss ein Wörterbuch oder ein Glossar benutzen.
17. Ist es maskulin oder feminin oder neutral, singular oder plural?
18. Als ist „ when " in der Vergangenheit.

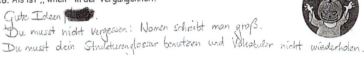

Gute Ideen

Du musst nicht vergessen: Nomen schreibt man groß.

Du musst dein Strukturenglossar benutzen und Vokabular nicht wiederholen.

GCSE Text	Inhalt [/15]	Sprache [/10]	Rechtschreibung und Grammatik [/5]
A*/A	• Total relevant mit vielen Details. Fast alle Informationen und Ideen sind entwickelt und total klar. • Meinungen (ein Minimum von 2). Sie sind detailliert und erklärt. • Der Text ist sehr gut strukturiert. [13-15 Punkte]	• Es gibt drei oder mehr Zeitformen. • Es gibt viele akkurate, komplexe Strukturen. • Es gibt sehr viele Konnektive. • Es gibt den Subjunktiv oder idiomatische Phrasen. • Es gibt viel interessantes, originelles Vokabular und keine Wiederholungen. [9-10 Punkte]	• Es ist meistens total akurat. • Es gibt nur Fehler in komplexen Strukturen. • Verben und Zeitformen sind akkurat. [5 Punkte]
B	• **Meistens** relevant und viele Informationen und Ideen sind klar. • Meinungen sind erklärt (ein Minimum von 2) • Man kann alles vertehen ohne die Überschriften zu lesen. [11-12 Punkte]	• Es gibt zwei Zeitformen. • Es gibt einige komplexe Strukturen und sie sind meistens akkurat. • Es gibt ziemlich viel interessantes Vokabular. • Es gibt einige Wiederholungen. [7-8 Punkte]	• Es gibt einige Fehler, aber es ist meistens akkurat. • Der Inhalt ist klar. • Verben und Zeitformen sind meistens akkurat. [4 Punkte]
C	• Ziemlich viele Informationen sind klar und relevant. • Manche Ideen sind entwickelt ,aber nicht alle. • Es gibt zwei Meinungen mit komplexen Strukturen. • Der Text ist nicht gut strukturiert und man muss die Überschriften lesen um den Text zu verstehen. [9-10 Punkte]	• Es gibt keine Variation von Konnektiven. • Komplexe Strukturen sind nicht immer akkurat. • Es gibt interessantes Vokabular, aber auch Wiederholungen. [5-6 Punkte]	• Es ist mehr akkurat als inakkurat, aber es gibt Fehler. • Der Inhalt ist oft klar, aber nicht immer. • Verben und Zeitformen sind manchmal inakkurat. [3 Punkte]
D and below	• Es gibt nicht so viele Details, aber manche Informationen und Ideen sind relevant. • Manche Ideen sind ein bisschen entwickelt. • Es gibt einfache Meinungen (mindestens 2). • Der Text ist nicht gut strukturiert. [0-8 Punkte]	• Das Vokabular ist sehr einfach. • Die Phrasen sind nicht komplex und zu kurz. • Die Phrasen sind nicht akkurat. • Es gibt viele Wiederholungen. [0-4 Punkte]	• Es gibt viele Fehler. • Der Inhalt ist nicht sehr klar. • Verben und Zeitformen sind oft inakkurat. [2 Punkte]

Meine Note: 20 **/30** A*=28+   A=26-27   B=22-25   C=17-21   D und darunter=0-16

Figure 8.3: Self-assessment sheet (*Selbstevaluationsblatt*)

Marian Carty and Judith Rifeser

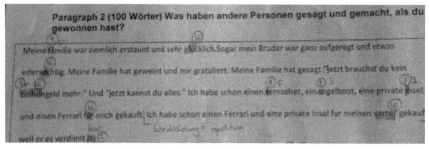

Figure 8.4: Marked first draft of pupil's written work

Figure 8.4 is an example of a first draft. The numbers relate to the common mistakes as shown in Figure 8.3 under '*Man muss nicht vergessen*'. Ticks and double ticks are used to acknowledge good and excellent work.

A collaborative writing task in the same format and with these feedback strategies would precede this individual work. We regularly plan collaborative writing tasks, which integrate speaking, listening, reading and writing in lessons to emphasize the importance of planning, drafting and redrafting written work. When writing in collaboration with their peers, learners are more likely to experiment with 'new syntactic forms' (Storch, 2011: 276). Writing tasks allow learners time to reflect, and collaborative writing enables them to discuss appropriate structures, negotiate meaning and share and consolidate their linguistic knowledge and skills. The result is not only better quality output but also allows pupils to 'process language more deeply, notice gaps in their interlanguage and reflect on language use' (ibid.).

Once pupils have re-drafted their work, they receive further feedback (Figure 8.5) that is both motivational but also includes an additional comment for improvement, to challenge them to further improve their work. It is also used for teachers to understand which mistakes the pupils did not manage to correct, which in turn provides feedback for the teacher to identify the areas that need to be addressed in future lessons.

However, it became evident that, to be able build explicit grammatical knowledge and understanding at KS4, action needed to be taken also at KS3. Pupils at KS3 needed to be exposed to grammar points, allowing them to make mistakes and start to use limited amounts of metalanguage to gradually move toward explicit knowledge. During this transition phase, grammar elements needed to be introduced into KS3 to raise 'grammatical awareness through guided exploration' (Harris *et al.*, 2001).

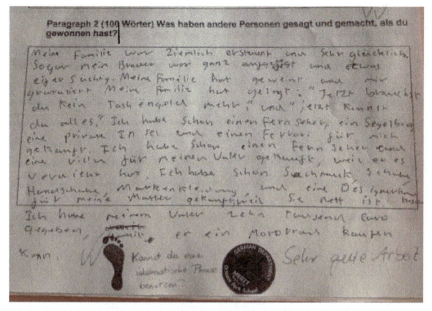

Figure 8.5: Re-drafted pupil written work

Grammar

Y8 German: Consolidating the use of "weil/ obwohl/selbst wenn"

('Because/although/even if … kicks the verb to the end')

Figure 8.6: Grammar song

Figure 8.6 shows an example of a song (to the tune of *Frère Jacques*) from the repertoire of songs and games with a clear grammatical focus that are used regularly to assist memorization of rules. An important moment occurred in a Year 8 German class that underpins the value of such memory hooks: after a formative assessment, a pupil approached me and said he was disappointed that his use of the conjunction '*dass*' (that) had been highlighted as incorrect in the sentences he had written. He explained that I had made the mistake of having omitted '*dass*' in the song (Figure 8.6). He suggested I include it immediately in the song so that he and his peers would not make the mistake again. As a result of situations like this, in which we encountered students repeatedly making very similar mistakes across the key stages, we made a list of their common errors and misconceptions more generally, and another list specific to each language. We then displayed key grammar rules (Figure 8.1) on the walls and, following on from this, devised the KS4 criteria (Figure 8.3). These were translated into the TL using simple and accessible questions. Figure 8.7 is the German version used at KS3.

For many, learning grammar can be bewildering or frustrating. Explaining grammar, whether in English or the TL, can be too complicated; often there are new concepts to understand, specific and numerous metalinguistic terms to be taught, explanations and rules to learn – all of which are often too great a burden on the memory. We need to plan for progression in the building of concepts, recognizing which ones are new and potentially difficult and which are similar in English. To address this, one might consider:

- planning for progression in teaching the language to talk about language and to discuss progress
- presenting rules simply and memorably once pupils have been using the language with confidence
- being selective and economical when planning to use and using metalanguage
- introducing metalanguage incrementally, building concepts gradually.

Die Wortstellung	Word order
1.Ist das Verb **am Ende** nach "weil /obwohl/dass/da/wenn"? 2."Denn"/"aber" kicken das Verb **nicht**. Hast du es richtig? 3.Ist das Verb die zweite Idee? 4.Ist das Partizip **am Ende**? 5.Ist der Infinitiv **am Ende**?	1.Is the verb at the end after "because/although/ that/if/when"? 2."Then"/ "but" don't kick the verb. Do you have it right? 3.Is the verb the second idea? 4.Is the past participle at the end? 5.Is the infinitive at the end?
Rechtschreibung	Spelling
6.Ist das Wort akkurat? 7.Ist es **ie** oder **ei**? 8.Hat das Wort einen Umlaut: ä ö ü? 9.Ist es **sh** oder **sch**? 10.Hast du ein Wort vergessen? (kann / hat /ist ...)	6.Is the word accurate? 7.Is it **ie** or **ei**? 8.Does the word have an umlaut ä ö ü? 9.Is it **sh** or **sch**? 10.Did you forget a word? (can/has/is...)
Verben und Zeitformen **Das Präsens** 11.Ist die Verbendung akkurat? (ich bin/ er/sie ist/ wir sind / ich denke / du denkst /er/sie denkt /wir denken/ ich war/ wir waren) **Das Perfekt** 12.Ist das Partizip mit **haben**? 13.Ist das Partizip mit **sein**? 14. Ist das **Hilfsverb** richtig? 15. Endet das Partizip mit t oder mit **en**? 16. Beginnt das Partizip mit **ge / be / ver** ...? 17. Das Partizip ist nicht normal. Was ist es? **Das Futur** 18.Ist die Form von **werden** richtig? (ich werde/ du wirst / er/sie/es wird / wir werden / ihr werdet / sie/Sie werden) 19.Ist es ein Infinitiv? **Modalverben** 20.Ist das erste Verb richtig? Ich darf / er muss/ wir können 21.Ist das zweite Verb ein Infinitiv? 22.Ist der Infinitiv am Ende?	Verbs and tenses **The Present tense** 11.Is the verb ending accurate? (**I** am/ he/she is/ we are/ I think/ you think/ she/she thinks/ we think/ I was/ we were **The perfect tense** 12.Is the participle with **to have**? 13.Is the participle with **to be**? 14. Is the **auxiliary verb** correct? 15.Does the participle end in t or **en**? 16.Does the participle begin with **ge / be / ver** ...? 17.The participle is not normal. What is it? **The Future tense** 18.Is the form of "will" correct? (I will/ you will / he/she/it will/ we will/ you plural will/ they/you formal will) 19.Is it an infinitive? **Modal verbs** 20. Is the first verb correct? (I may/ he must/ we can) 21. Is the second verb an infinitive? 22. Is the infinitive at the end?
Negative	Negatives
23.Ist es kein / keinen / keine / kein oder keine? 24. Ist es kein (e)(en) oder nicht?	23. Is it "not a" (nom masc/accu masc/ fem/neut or plural? 24. Is "not a" accusative neut/fem/masc or not?
Nomen und Artikel	Nouns and articles
25.Hast du das Nomen **groß** geschrieben? (Punkte, Mutter, Freundin) 26.Ist es Singular oder Plural? 27.Ist es der /die / das oder die? 28.Ist es ein / eine /ein (mein /meine /mein /meine)?	25.Have you written the noun with a **capital letter**? (points, mother, (girl)friend) 26.Is it singular or plural? 27.Is it "the" masc/fem/neut or plural? 28.Is it "a" masc/fem/neut ("my" masc/fem/neut/plural)?
Adjektive	Adjectives
29.Ist die Adjektivendung richtig? 30.Hast du den Komparativ richtig geschrieben? (besser als, musikalischer als) 31.Hast du den Superlativ richtig geschrieben? (**am besten**)	29.Is the adjective ending correct? 30. Have you used the comparative correctly? (better than, **more** musical than) 31. Have you used the superlative correctly? (the best)
Satzzeichen	Punctuation
32. Hast du einen Punkt (.) vergessen? 33. Hast du ein Komma (,) vergessen? 34. Hast du ein Fragezeichen (?) vergessen? 35. Hast du einen Doppelpunkt (:) vergessen? 36. Sind die Anführungszeichen richtig?	32. Have you forgotten a full stop (.) ? 33. Have you forgotten a comma (,) ? 34. Have you forgotten a question mark (?) ? 35. Have you forgotten a colon (:) ? 36. Are the inverted commas right?

Figure 8.7: Target language grammar prompt sheet

Raising grammatical awareness through guided exploration			
Implicit			Explicit
	Learners use language regularly orally		
	⟵⟶		
Stage 1	Stage 2	Stage 3	Stage 4
No reflection	Is it X or Y?	What is ...?	Why is it ...?
Phrase used as a memorised chunk	Prompted closed reflection	Teacher or learner draws attention to differences	Teacher or learner asks for explanation
On va chanter	C'est on va chanter ou on va chante?	C'est quoi la terminaison?	Pourquoi c'est chanter et non pas chante?
Wir werden singen	Was ist richtig? Wir werden singe oder wir werden singen?	Was ist die Endung?	Warum ist es singen und nicht singe?
Vamos a cantar	¿Es vamos a canta o vamos a cantar?	¿Cuál es la terminación?	¿Por qué es vamos a cantar y no vamos a canta?

Figure 8.8: The journey from the implicit to the explicit

Figure 8.8, adapted from Harris *et al.* (2001: 113) shows the journey from implicit to explicit grammar learning that is key to context-embedded assessment for learning. It outlines the stages of raising grammatical awareness using simple and accessible language that can be implemented at KS3, as well as examples of pupils' mistakes. It is essential that the application and discussion of these grammatical concepts arise from the pupils' own work, to provide a meaningful context.

In Figure 8.9 you will see that the language listed is relatively simple and transferable to diverse contexts, and contains no metalanguage.

Pour parler de la grammaire en français	Para hablar de la gramática en español	Um über die Grammatik auf Deutsch zu sprechen
C'est … Ce n'est pas … correct/possible/normal/une letter phantom/comme/ identique/similaire	Es … no es … correcto/ normal/posible	Das ist richtig/falsch.
		Das ist nicht richtig.
	Es como …	
Ce n'est pas X … c'est Y.	No es X … es Y.	Das ist möglich/ unmöglich/ nicht möglich.
Quelle est la différence entre … et …?	¿Cuál es la diferencia?	… ist (k)ein …
	La terminación es …	Es ist wie …
Il y a … Il n'y a pas de …	¡Para! ¡Hay un problema!	Es gibt (k)ein …
Ça change … Ça ne change pas.	¿Por qué … ? Porque …	Es beginnt/endet mit …
Ça commence/finit par …	¿Cómo se dice … en español?	Die Endung ist …
La terminaison est …	¿De qué color es?	Stop! Es gibt einen Fehler/ein Problem mit …!
Stop! Il y a une erreur/un problème avec …	No lo sé/lo sé.	Es fehlt …
Pourquoi? Parce que …	Falta …	Warum? Weil …
Comment dit-on … en français?		Wie sagt man … auf Deutsch?
Combien?		Wieviele …?
C'est quelle couleur?		Welche Farbe hat …?
Je suis d'accord/ Je ne suis pas d'accord.		
Je ne sais pas. C'est comme ça!		
Il faut l'accepter.		

Figure 8.9: Target language grammar phrases

Finally, at the end of the project, pupils in KS4 were asked to give feedback on how they felt the new AfL strategies and self-assessment sheets were helping them in their learning:

> 'The numbers are very useful. I can see what I have done wrong though the numbers, so number 9 will be like "You must put the verb at the end". It is very useful and improves my learning. It also helps me to get work back quicker so we have more time to improve.'

> (Year 10 pupil, GCSE Predicted Grade B)

'I think that the new system of marking is beneficial because you can learn by correcting your own mistakes instead of the teachers correcting it for you. I now think about how to correct the sentences and what I did wrong rather than just looking at the correction already given.'

(Year 10 pupil, GCSE Predicted Grade A)

'It's really good and helps me see where I have gone wrong and how to correct it. It made me write more complex German.'

(Year 10 pupil, GCSE Predicted Grade C)

Implications for future practice

These are some of the questions we are now considering as a result of the project:

- How can we ensure that assessment for learning tasks offer a genuine challenge in the thoughtful and effective use of the language students have been learning in a context which they regard as meaningful?
- How we can we motivate students through engaging assessment activities to want to improve their linguistic competence for its own sake and a love of learning?
- How can we translate this meaningful information, which is valid in the learners' eyes, into data that is more holistic and less reductive than a mere number?

Further reading

Black, P. and Jones, J. (2006) 'Formative assessment and the learning and teaching of MFL: Sharing the language learning road map with the learners'. *The Language Learning Journal,* 34 (1), 4–9.

Black , P. and Wiliam, D. (1998) 'Assessment and classroom learning'. *Assessment in Education: Principles, Policy & Practice,* 5 (1), 7–73.

Wiliam, D. (2011) *Embedded Formative Assessment.* Bloomington, IN: Solution Tree Press.

Acknowledgements

All of the examples presented have come from the work of the MFL department in Orleans Park. However, the evolution of this department has come about, and continues to develop, as a result of collaboration not only within the department but also with university PGCE tutors and colleagues from a number of schools within the PGCE partnership. The collaboration has included in-class coaching involving university PGCE tutors; observation and feedback from MFL colleagues across the PGCE partnership; and close liaison with PGCE students and PGCE tutors to develop schemes of work. PGCE students have played a pivotal role in sourcing exciting, linguistically accessible authentic material (feature films, short films and songs of many genres), which pupils find highly engaging.

With thanks to Elaine Ball, headteacher at Orleans Park; Hana Sheikh and Janet Livesey, assistant headteachers; Laura Mosley, head of department; Chris Hill, second in department; Anna Parkes, previous head of French and second in department; and all other colleagues of the MFL department.

References

Christie, C. (2013) 'Speaking spontaneously in the modern foreign languages classroom: Tools for supporting successful target language conversation'. *Language Learning Journal*, 44 (1), 1–16.

— (2013) *Interact! Learning through spontaneous speaking in modern languages.* Cumbria: Cumbria Publishing.

Council for Cultural Co-operation (2001) *Common European Framework of Reference for Languages: Learning, teaching, assessment.* Cambridge: CUP.

Doughty, C. and Williams, J. (1998) *Focus on Form in Classroom Second Language Acquisition.* Cambridge: CUP.

Harris, V., Burch, J., Jones, B. and Darcy, J. (2001) *Something to Say?* London: CILT.

Johnson, K. (2001) *An Introduction to Foreign Language Learning and Teaching.* Harlow: Pearson Education Ltd.

Kohn, A. (2011) 'The case against grades'. *Educational Leadership.* Online. www.alfiekohn.org/article/case-grades (accessed 3 July 2016).

Krashen, S. and Terrell, T.D. (1983) *The Natural Approach: Language acquisition in the classroom.* Oxford: Pergamon.

Lawes, S. (2000) 'The unique contribution of modern foreign languages to the curriculum'. In Field, K. (ed.) *Issues in Modern Foreign Languages Teaching.* Abingdon: Routledge.

Little, D. (1991) *Learner Autonomy 1: Definitions, issues and problems.* Dublin: Authentik.

Long, M.H. (1991) 'Focus On Form: A design feature in language teaching methodology'. In DeBot, K., Ginsberg, R. and Kramsch, C. (eds.), *Foreign Language Research in Crosscultural Perspective.* Amsterdam: John Benjamins.

— (1988) 'Instructed Interlanguage Development'. In Beebe, L. (ed), *Issues In Second Language Acquisition: Multiple perspectives.* Rowley, MA: Newbury House.

Mitchell, R. (2011) 'Still Gardening In A Gale: Policy, research and practice in foreign language education in England'. *FLuL,* 40 (1), 1–19.

— (2003) 'Rethinking the concept of progression in the National Curriculum for Modern Foreign Languages: A research perspective'. *Language Learning Journal,* 27 (1), 15–23.

— (1994) 'The Communicative Approach To Language Teaching: An introduction'. In A. Swarbrick (ed.) *Teaching Modern Languages*. London: Routledge.

Myles, F. (1998) 'Rote or rule? Exploring the role of formulaic language in classroom foreign language learning'. *Language Learning*, 48 (3), 323–63.

Ofsted (2011) *Modern Languages Achievement and Challenge 2007–2010*. No. 100042. Online. www.gov.uk/government/uploads/system/uploads/attachment_data/file/413782/Modern_languages_achievement_and_challenge_2007-2010.pdf (accessed 4 September 2015).

Pachler, N., Evans, M. and Lawes, S. (2005) *Modern Foreign Languages: Teaching school subjects 11–19*. London: RoutledgeFalmer.

Storch, S. (2011) 'Collaborative writing in L2 contexts: Processes, outcomes, and future directions'. *Annual Review of Applied Linguistics,* 31, 275–88.

Swain, M. (1985) 'Communicative Competence: Some roles of comprehensible input and comprehensible output in its development'. In Gass, S and Madden, C. (eds), *Input In Second Language Acquisition*. Rowley, MA: Newbury House.

Widdowson, H.G. (1990) *Aspects of Language Teaching*. Oxford: Oxford University Press.

Wiliam, D. (2009). *Assessment for Learning: Why, what and how?* London: Institute of Education.

Yandell, J. (2013) 'Curriculum pedagogy and assessment: Of rigour and unfinished revolutions'. In Allen, M. and Ainley, P. (eds), *Education Beyond the Coalition: Reclaiming the agenda*. Online. https://radicaledbks.files.wordpress.com/2013/09/john-yandell-pedagogy.pdf (accessed 16 March 2016).